CENTURY OF
LIGHT

Bahá'í Publishing Trust
Wilmette, Illinois 60091-2886

A Publication of
The Universal House of Justice

ISBN 0-87743-294-5

Printed in the United States of America

FOREWORD

The conclusion of the twentieth century provides Bahá'ís with a unique vantage point. During the past hundred years our world underwent changes far more profound than any in its preceding history, changes that are, for the most part, little understood by the present generation. These same hundred years saw the Bahá'í Cause emerge from obscurity, demonstrating on a global scale the unifying power with which its Divine origin has endowed it. As the century drew to its close, the convergence of these two historical developments became increasingly apparent.

Century of Light, prepared under our supervision, reviews these two processes and the relationship between them, in the context of the Bahá'í Teachings. We commend it to the thoughtful study of the friends, in the confidence that the perspectives it opens up will prove both spiritually enriching and of practical help in sharing with others the challenging implications of the Revelation brought by Bahá'u'lláh.

THE UNIVERSAL HOUSE OF JUSTICE

Naw-Rúz, 158 B.E.

CENTURY OF LIGHT

THE TWENTIETH CENTURY, the most turbulent in the history of the human race, has reached its end. Dismayed by the deepening moral and social chaos that marked its course, the generality of the world's peoples are eager to leave behind them the memories of the suffering that these decades brought with them. No matter how frail the foundations of confidence in the future may seem, no matter how great the dangers looming on the horizon, humanity appears desperate to believe that, through some fortuitous conjunction of circumstances, it will nevertheless be possible to bend the conditions of human life into conformity with prevailing human desires.

In the light of the teachings of Bahá'u'lláh such hopes are not merely illusory, but miss entirely the nature and meaning of the great turning point through which our world has passed in these crucial hundred years. Only as humanity comes to understand the implications of what occurred during this period of history will it be able to meet the challenges that lie ahead. The value of the contribution we as Bahá'ís can make to the process demands that we ourselves grasp the significance of the historic transformation wrought by the twentieth century.

What makes this insight possible for us is the light shed by the rising Sun of Bahá'u'lláh's Revelation and the influence it has come to exercise in human affairs. It is this opportunity that the following pages address.

I

LET US ACKNOWLEDGE AT THE OUTSET the magnitude of the ruin that the human race has brought upon itself during the period of history under review. The loss of life alone has been beyond counting. The disintegration of basic institutions of social order, the violation—indeed, the abandonment—of standards of decency, the betrayal of the life of the mind through surrender to ideologies as squalid as they have been empty, the invention and deployment of monstrous weapons of mass annihilation, the bankrupting of entire nations and the reduction of masses of human beings to hopeless poverty, the reckless destruction of the environment of the planet—such are only the more obvious in a catalogue of horrors unknown to even the darkest of ages past. Merely to mention them is to call to mind the Divine warnings expressed in Bahá'u'lláh's words of a century ago: "O heedless ones! Though the wonders of My mercy have encompassed all created things, both visible and invisible, and though the revelations of My grace and bounty have permeated every atom of the universe, yet the rod with which I can chastise the wicked is grievous, and the fierceness of Mine anger against them terrible."[1]

Lest any observer of the Cause be tempted to misunderstand such warnings as only metaphorical, Shoghi Effendi, drawing some of the historical implications, wrote in 1941:

A tempest, unprecedented in its violence, unpredictable in its course, catastrophic in its immediate effects, unimaginably glorious in its ultimate consequences, is at present sweeping the face of the earth. Its driving power is remorselessly gaining in range and momentum. Its cleansing force, however much undetected, is increasing with every passing day. Humanity, gripped in the clutches of its devastating power, is smitten by the evidences of its resistless fury. It can neither perceive its origin, nor probe its significance, nor discern its outcome. Bewildered, agonized and helpless, it watches this great and mighty wind of God invading the remotest and fairest regions of the earth, rocking its foundations, deranging its equilibrium, sundering its nations, disrupting the homes of its peoples, wasting its cities, driving into exile its kings, pulling down its bulwarks, uprooting its institutions, dimming its light, and harrowing up the souls of its inhabitants.[2]

✻

From the point of view of wealth and influence, "the world" of 1900 was Europe and, by grudging concession, the United States. Throughout the planet, Western imperialism was pursuing among the populations of other lands what it regarded as its "civilizing mission". In the words of one historian, the century's opening decade appeared to be essentially a continuation of the "long nineteenth century",[3] an era whose boundless self-satisfaction was perhaps best epitomized by the celebration in 1897 of Queen Victoria's diamond jubilee, a parade that rolled for hours through the streets of London, with an imperial panoply and display of military power far surpassing anything attempted in past civilizations.

As the century began, there were few, whatever their degree of social or moral sensitivity, who perceived the catastrophes lying ahead, and few, if any, who could have conceived their magnitude. The military leadership of most European nations assumed that war of some kind would break out, but viewed the prospect with equanimity because of the twin fixed convictions that it would be short and would be won by their side.

To an extent that seemed little short of miraculous, the international peace movement was enlisting the support of statesmen, industrialists, scholars, the media, and influential personalities as unlikely as the tsar of Russia. If the inordinate increase in armaments seemed ominous, the network of painstakingly crafted and often overlapping alliances seemed to give assurance that a general conflagration would be avoided and regional disputes settled, as they had been through most of the previous century. This illusion was reinforced by the fact that Europe's crowned heads— most of them members of one extended family, and many of them exercising seemingly decisive political power—addressed one another familiarly by nicknames, carried on an intimate correspondence, married one another's sisters and daughters, and vacationed together throughout long stretches of each year at one another's castles, regattas and shooting lodges. Even the painful disparities in the distribution of wealth were being energetically—if not very systematically—addressed in Western societies through legislation designed to restrain the worst of the corporate freebooting of preceding decades and to meet the most urgent demands of growing urban populations.

The vast majority of the human family, living in lands outside the Western world, shared in few of the blessings and little of the optimism of their European and American brethren. China, despite its ancient civilization and its sense of itself as the "Middle Kingdom", had become the hapless victim of plundering by Western nations and by its modernizing neighbour Japan. The multitudes in India—whose economy and political life had fallen so totally under the domination of a single imperial power as to exclude the usual jockeying for advantage—escaped some of the worst of the abuses afflicting other lands, but watched impotently as their desperately needed resources were drained away. The coming agony of Latin America was all too clearly prefigured in the suffering of Mexico, large sections of which had been annexed by its great northern neighbour, and whose natural resources were already attracting the attention of avaricious foreign corporations. Particularly embarrassing from a Western point of view—because of its proximity to such brilliant European capitals as Berlin and Vienna—was the medieval oppression in which the hundred million nominally liberated serfs in

Russia led lives of sullen, hopeless misery. Most tragic of all was the plight of the inhabitants of the African continent, divided against one another by artificial boundaries created through cynical bargains among European powers. It has been estimated that during the first decade of the twentieth century over a million people in the Congo perished— starved, beaten, worked literally to death for the profit of their distant masters, a preview of the fate that was to engulf well over one hundred million of their fellow human beings across Europe and Asia before the century reached its end.[4]

These masses of humankind, despoiled and scorned—but representing most of the earth's inhabitants—were seen not as protagonists but essentially as objects of the new century's much vaunted civilizing process. Despite benefits conferred on a minority among them, the colonial peoples existed chiefly to be acted upon—to be used, trained, exploited, Christianized, civilized, mobilized—as the shifting agendas of Western powers dictated. These agendas may have been harsh or mild in execution, enlightened or selfish, evangelical or exploitative, but were shaped by materialistic forces that determined both their means and most of their ends. To a large extent, religious and political pieties of various kinds masked both ends and means from the publics in Western lands, who were thus able to derive moral satisfaction from the blessings their nations were assumed to be conferring on less worthy peoples, while themselves enjoying the material fruits of this benevolence.

To point out the failings of a great civilization is not to deny its accomplishments. As the twentieth century opened, the peoples of the West could take justifiable pride in the technological, scientific and philosophical developments for which their societies had been responsible. Decades of experimentation had placed in their hands material means that were still beyond the appreciation of the rest of humanity. Throughout both Europe and America vast industries had risen, dedicated to metallurgy, to the manufacturing of chemical products of every kind, to textiles, to construction and to the production of instruments that enhanced every aspect of life. A continuous process of discovery, design and improvement was making accessible power of unimaginable magnitude—with, alas, ecological consequences equally unimagined at the time—especially through the use of cheap fuel and electricity. The "era of the railroad" was far advanced and steamships coursed the seaways of the world. With the proliferation of telegraph and telephone communication, Western society anticipated the moment when it would be freed of the limiting effects that geographical distances had imposed on humankind since the dawn of history.

Changes taking place at the deeper level of scientific thought were even more far-reaching in their implications. The nineteenth century had still been held in the grip of the Newtonian view of the world as a vast clockwork system, but by the end of the century the intellectual strides necessary to challenge that view had already been taken. New ideas were emerging that would lead to the formulation of quantum mechanics; and before long the revolutionizing effect of the theory of relativity would call into question beliefs about the phenomenal world that had been accepted as common sense for centuries. Such breakthroughs were encouraged—and their influence greatly amplified—by the fact that science had already changed from an activity of isolated thinkers to the systematically pursued concern of a large and influential international community enjoying the amenities of universities, laboratories and symposia for the exchange of experimental discoveries.

Nor was the strength of Western societies limited to scientific and technological advances. As the twentieth century opened, Western civilization was reaping the fruits of a philosophical culture that was rapidly liberating the energies of its populations, and whose influence would soon produce a revolutionary impact throughout the entire world. It was a culture which nurtured constitutional government, prized the rule of law and respect for the rights of all of society's members, and held up to the eyes of all it reached a vision of a coming age of social justice. If the boasts of liberty and equality that inflated patriotic rhetoric in Western lands were a far cry from conditions actually prevailing, Westerners could justly celebrate the advances toward those ideals that had been accomplished in the nineteenth century.

From a spiritual perspective the age was gripped by a strange, paradoxical duality. In almost every direction the intellectual horizon was darkened by clouds of superstition produced by unthinking imitation of earlier ages. For most of the world's peoples, the consequences ranged from profound ignorance about both human potentialities and the physical universe, to naïve attachment to theologies that bore little or no relation to experience. Where winds of change did dispel the mists, among the educated classes in Western lands, inherited orthodoxies were all too often replaced by the blight of an aggressive secularism that called into doubt both the spiritual nature of humankind and the authority of moral values themselves. Everywhere, the secularization of society's upper levels seemed to go hand in hand with a pervasive religious obscurantism among the general population. At the deepest level—because religion's influence reaches far into the human psyche and claims for itself a unique kind of authority—religious prejudices in all lands had kept alive in successive generations smouldering fires of bitter animosity that would fuel the horrors of the coming decades.[5]

II

ON THIS LANDSCAPE OF FALSE CONFIDENCE and deep despair, of scientific enlightenment and spiritual gloom, there appeared, as the twentieth century opened, the luminous figure of 'Abdu'l-Bahá. The journey that had brought Him to this pivotal moment in the history of humankind had led through more than fifty years of exile, imprisonment and privation, hardly a month having passed in anything that resembled tranquillity and ease. He came to it resolved to proclaim to responsive and heedless alike the establishment on earth of that promised reign of universal peace and justice that had sustained human hope throughout the centuries. Its foundation, He declared, would be the unification, in this "century of light", of the world's people:

> In this day ... means of communication have multiplied, and the five continents of the earth have virtually merged into one.... In like manner all the members of the human family, whether peoples or governments, cities or villages, have become increasingly interdependent.... Hence the unity of all mankind can in this day be achieved. Verily this is none other but one of the wonders of this wondrous age, this glorious century.[6]

During the long years of imprisonment and banishment that followed Bahá'u'lláh's refusal to serve the political agenda of the
Ottoman authorities, 'Abdu'l-Bahá was entrusted with the management of the Faith's affairs and with the responsibility of acting as His
Father's spokesman. A significant aspect of this work entailed interaction with local and provincial officials who sought His advice on
the problems confronting them. Not dissimilar needs presented themselves in the Master's homeland. As early as 1875, responding to
Bahá'u'lláh's instructions, 'Abdu'l-Bahá addressed to the rulers and
people of Persia a treatise entitled *The Secret of Divine Civilization*,
setting out the spiritual principles that must guide the shaping of
their society in the age of humanity's maturity. Its opening passage
called upon the Iranian people to reflect on the lesson taught by history about the key to social progress:

> Consider carefully: all these highly varied phenomena, these con-
> cepts, this knowledge, these technical procedures and philosophical
> systems, these sciences, arts, industries and inventions—all are ema-
> nations of the human mind. Whatever people has ventured deeper
> into this shoreless sea, has come to excel the rest. The happiness and
> pride of a nation consist in this, that it should shine out like the sun
> in the high heaven of knowledge. "Shall they who have knowledge
> and they who have it not, be treated alike?"[7]

The Secret of Divine Civilization presaged the guidance that would flow
from the pen of 'Abdu'l-Bahá in subsequent decades. After the devastating
loss that followed the ascension of Bahá'u'lláh, the Persian believers were
revived and heartened by a flood of Tablets from the Master, which provided not only the spiritual sustenance they needed, but leadership in
finding their way through the turmoil that was undermining the established order of things in their land. These communications, reaching even
the smallest villages across the country, responded to the appeals and questions of countless individual believers, bringing guidance, encouragement
and assurance. We read, for example, a Tablet addressing believers in the
village of Kishih, mentioning by name nearly one hundred and sixty of
them. Of the age now dawning, the Master says: "this is the century of

light," explaining that the meaning of this image is acceptance of the principle of oneness and its implications:

> My meaning is that the beloved of the Lord must regard every ill-wisher as a well-wisher.… That is, they must associate with a foe as befitteth a friend, and deal with an oppressor as beseemeth a kind companion. They should not gaze upon the faults and transgressions of their foes, nor pay heed to their enmity, inequity or oppression.[8]

Extraordinarily, the small company of persecuted believers, living in this remote corner of a land which still remained largely unaffected by the developments taking place elsewhere in social and intellectual life, are summoned by this Tablet to raise their eyes above the level of local concerns and to see the implications of unity on a global scale:

> Rather, should they view people in the light of the Blessed Beauty's call that the entire human race are servants of the Lord of might and glory, as He hath brought the whole creation under the purview of His gracious utterance, and hath enjoined upon us to show forth love and affection, wisdom and compassion, faithfulness and unity towards all, without any discrimination.[9]

Here, the call of the Master is not only to a new level of understanding, but implies the need for commitment and action. In the urgency and confidence of the language it employs can be felt the power that would produce the great achievements of the Persian believers in the decades since then—both in the world-wide promotion of the Cause and in the acquisition of capacities that advance civilization:

> O ye beloved of the Lord! With the utmost joy and gladness, serve ye the human world, and love ye the human race. Turn your eyes away from limitations, and free yourselves from restrictions, for … freedom therefrom brings about divine blessings and bestowals.

> Wherefore, rest ye not, be it for an instant; seek ye not a minute's respite nor a moment's repose. Surge ye even as the billows of a mighty sea, and roar like unto the leviathan of the ocean of eternity.

Therefore, so long as there be a trace of life in one's veins, one must strive and labour, and seek to lay a foundation that the passing of centuries and cycles may not undermine, and rear an edifice which the rolling of ages and aeons cannot overthrow—an edifice that shall prove eternal and everlasting, so that the sovereignty of heart and soul may be established and secure in both worlds.[10]

Social historians of the future, with a perspective far more dispassionate and universal than is presently possible, and benefiting from unimpeded access to all of the primary documentation, will study minutely the transformation that the Master achieved in these early years. Day after day, month after month, from a distant exile where He was endlessly harried by the host of enemies surrounding Him, 'Abdu'l-Bahá was able not only to stimulate the expansion of the Persian Bahá'í community, but to shape its consciousness and collective life. The result was the emergence of a culture, however localized, that was unlike anything humanity had ever known. Our century, with all its upheavals and its grandiloquent claims to create a new order, has no comparable example of the systematic application of the powers of a single Mind to the building of a distinctive and successful community that saw its ultimate sphere of work as the globe itself.

Although suffering intermittent atrocities at the hands of the Muslim clergy and their supporters—without protection from a succession of indolent Qájár monarchs—the Persian Bahá'í community found a new lease on life. The number of believers multiplied in all regions of the country, persons prominent in the life of society were enrolled, including several influential members of the clergy, and the forerunners of administrative institutions emerged in the form of rudimentary consultative bodies. The importance of the latter development alone would be impossible to exaggerate. In a land and among a people accustomed for centuries to a patriarchal system that concentrated all decision-making authority in the hands of an absolute monarch or Shí'ih mujtáhids, a community representing a cross section of that society had broken with the past, taking into its own hands the responsibility for deciding its collective affairs through consultative action.

In the society and culture the Master was developing, spiritual energies expressed themselves in the practical affairs of day-to-day life. The emphasis in the teachings on education provided the impulse for the establishment of Bahá'í schools—including the Tarbíyat school for girls,[11] which gained national renown—in the capital, as well as in provincial centres. With the assistance of American and European Bahá'í helpers, clinics and other medical facilities followed. As early as 1925, communities in a number of cities had instituted classes in Esperanto, in response to their awareness of the Bahá'í teaching that some form of auxiliary international language must be adopted. A network of couriers, reaching across the land, provided the struggling Bahá'í community with the rudiments of the postal service that the rest of the country so conspicuously lacked. The changes under way touched the homeliest circumstances of day-to-day life. In obedience to the laws of the Kitáb-i-Aqdas, for example, Persian Bahá'ís abandoned the use of the filthy public baths, prolific in their spread of infection and disease, and began to rely on showers that used fresh water.

All of these advances, whether social, organizational or practical, owed their driving force to the moral transformation taking place among the believers, a transformation that was steadily distinguishing Bahá'ís—even in the eyes of those hostile to the Faith—as candidates for positions of trust. That such far-reaching changes could so quickly set one segment of the Persian population apart from the largely antagonistic majority around it was a demonstration of the powers released by Bahá'u'lláh's Covenant with His followers and by 'Abdu'l-Bahá's assumption of the leadership this Covenant invested uniquely in Him.

Throughout these years Persian political life was in almost constant turmoil. While Náṣiri'd-Dín Sháh's immediate successor, Muẓaffari'd-Dín Sháh, was induced to approve a constitution in 1906, his successor, Muḥammad-'Alí Sháh, recklessly dissolved the first two parliaments—in one case attacking with cannon fire the building where the legislature was meeting. The so-called "Constitutional Movement" that overthrew him and compelled the last of the Qájár kings, Aḥmad Sháh, to summon a third parliament was itself riven by competing factions and shamelessly manipulated by the Shí'ih clergy. Efforts by Bahá'ís to play a constructive role in this process of modernization were repeatedly frustrated by royalist and popular factions alike, both of which were inspired by the prevailing religious prejudice and saw in the Bahá'í community merely a convenient scapegoat. Here again, only a more politically mature age than our own will be able to appreciate the way in which the Master—setting an example for future challenges that the Bahá'í community must inevitably encounter—guided the beleaguered community in doing all it could to encourage political reform, and then in being willing to step aside when these efforts were cynically rebuffed.

It was not only through His Tablets that ʿAbdu'l-Bahá exercised this influence on the rapidly developing Bahá'í community in the cradle of the Faith. Unlike Westerners, Persian believers were not distinguished from other peoples of the Near East by dress and appearance, and so travellers from the cradle of the Faith did not arouse the suspicion of the Ottoman authorities. Consequently, a steady stream of Persian pilgrims provided ʿAbdu'l-Bahá with another powerful means of inspiring the friends, guiding their activities, and drawing them ever more deeply into an understanding of Bahá'u'lláh's purpose. Some of the greatest names in Persian Bahá'í history were among those who journeyed to ʿAkká and returned to their homes prepared to give their lives if necessary for the achievement of the Master's vision. The immortal Varqá and his son Rúḥu'lláh were among this privileged number, as were Ḥájí Mírzá Ḥaydar ʿAlí, Mírzá Abu'l Faḍl, Mírzá Muḥammad-Taqí Afnán and four distinguished Hands of the Cause, Ibn-i-Abhar, Ḥájí Mullá ʿAlí Akbar, Adíbu'l-Ulamá and Ibn-i-Aṣdaq. The spirit that today sustains Persian pioneers in every part of the world and that plays so creative a role in the building of Bahá'í community life runs like a straight line through family after family back to those heroic days. In retrospect, it is apparent that the phenomenon we today know as the twin processes of expansion and consolidation itself had its origin in those marvellous years.

Inspired by the Master's words and the accounts brought back from the Holy Land, Persian believers arose to undertake travel-teaching activities in the Far East. During the latter years of Bahá'u'lláh's Ministry, communities had been established in India and Burma, and the Faith carried as far as China; and this work was now reinforced. A demonstration of the new powers released in the Cause was the erection in the Russian province of Turkestan, where a vigorous Bahá'í community life had also developed, of the first Bahá'í House of Worship in the world,[12] a project inspired by the Master and guided, from its inception, by His advice.

It was this broad range of activities, carried out by an increasingly confident body of believers and stretching from the Mediterranean to the China Sea, that built the base of support from which 'Abdu'l-Bahá was able to pursue the promising opportunities which, as the new century opened, had already begun to unfold in the West. Not the least important feature of this base was its embrace of representatives of the Orient's great diversity of racial, religious and national backgrounds. This achievement provided 'Abdu'l-Bahá with the examples on which He would repeatedly draw in His proclamation to Western audiences of the integrating forces that had been released through Bahá'u'lláh's advent.

The greatest victory of these early years was the Master's success in constructing on Mount Carmel, on the spot designated for it by Bahá'u'lláh and through immense effort, a mausoleum for the remains of the Báb, which had been brought at great risk and difficulty to the Holy Land. Shoghi Effendi has explained that whereas in past ages the blood of martyrs was the seed of personal faith, in this day it has constituted the seed of the administrative institutions of the Cause.[13] Such an insight lends special meaning to the way in which the Administrative Centre of Bahá'u'lláh's World Order would take shape under the shadow of the Shrine of the Faith's Martyr-Prophet. Shoghi Effendi sets the Master's achievement in global and historical perspective:

> For, just as in the realm of the spirit, the reality of the Báb has been hailed by the Author of the Bahá'í Revelation as "the Point round Whom the realities of the Prophets and Messengers revolve," so, on this visible plane, His sacred remains constitute the heart and center of what may be regarded as nine concentric circles,[14] paralleling thereby, and adding further emphasis to the central position accorded by the Founder of our Faith to One "from Whom God hath caused to proceed the knowledge of all that was and shall be," "the Primal Point from which have been generated all created things."[15]

The significance in 'Abdu'l-Bahá's own eyes of the mission He had accomplished at such cost is movingly depicted by Shoghi Effendi:

> When all was finished, and the earthly remains of the Martyr-Prophet of <u>Sh</u>íráz were, at long last, safely deposited for their everlasting rest in the bosom of God's holy mountain, 'Abdu'l-Bahá, Who had cast aside His turban, removed His shoes and thrown off His cloak, bent low over the still open sarcophagus, His silver hair waving about His head and His face transfigured and luminous, rested His forehead on the border of the wooden casket, and, sobbing aloud, wept with such a weeping that all those who were present wept with Him. That night He could not sleep, so overwhelmed was He with emotion.[16]

By 1908, the so-called "Young Turk Revolution" had freed not only most of the Ottoman empire's political prisoners, but 'Abdu'l-Bahá as well. Suddenly, the restraints that had kept Him confined to the prison-city of 'Akká and its immediate surroundings had fallen away, and the Master was in a position to proceed with an enterprise that Shoghi Effendi was later to describe as one of the three principal achievements of His ministry: His public proclamation of the Cause of God in the great population centres of the Western world.

Because of the dramatic character of the events that occurred in North America and Europe, accounts of the Master's historic journeys sometimes tend to overlook the important opening year spent in Egypt. 'Abdu'l-Bahá arrived there in September 1910, intending to go on directly to Europe, but was compelled by illness to remain in residence at Ramleh, a suburb of Alexandria, until August of the following year. As it turned out, the months that followed were a period of great productivity whose full effects on the fortunes of the Cause, in the African continent especially, will be felt for many years to come. To some extent the way had no doubt been paved by warm admiration for the Master on the part of <u>Sh</u>ay<u>kh</u> Muḥammad 'Abduh, who had met Him on several occasions in Beirut and who subsequently became Mufti of Egypt and a leading figure at Al-Azhar University.

An aspect of the Egyptian sojourn that deserves special attention was the opportunity it provided for the first public proclamation of the Faith's message. The relatively cosmopolitan and liberal atmosphere prevailing in Cairo and Alexandria at the time opened a way for frank and searching discussions between the Master and prominent figures in the intellectual world of Sunni Islam. These included clerics, parliamentarians, administrators and aristocrats. Further, editors and journalists from influential Arabic-language newspapers, whose information about the Cause had been coloured by prejudiced reports emanating from Persia and Constantinople, now had an opportunity to learn the facts of the situation for themselves. Publications that had been openly hostile changed their tone. The editors of one such newspaper opened an article on the Master's arrival by referring to "His Eminence Mírzá 'Abbás Effendi, the learned and erudite Head of the Bahá'ís in 'Akká and the Centre of authority for Bahá'ís throughout the world" and expressing appreciation of His visit to Alexandria.[17] This and other articles paid particular tribute to 'Abdu'l-Bahá's understanding of Islam and to the principles of unity and religious tolerance that lay at the heart of His teachings.

Despite the Master's ill health that had caused it, the Egyptian interlude proved to be a great blessing. Western diplomats and officials were able to observe at first-hand the extraordinary success of 'Abdu'l-Bahá's interaction with leading figures in a region of the Near East that was of lively interest in European circles. Accordingly, by the time the Master embarked for Marseilles on 11 August 1911, His fame had preceded Him.

III

A TABLET ADDRESSED BY 'ABDU'L-BAHÁ to an American believer in 1905 contains a statement that is as illuminating as it is touching. Referring to His situation following the ascension of Bahá'u'lláh, 'Abdu'l-Bahá spoke of a letter He had received from America at "a time when an ocean of trials and tribulations was surging…":

> Such was our state when a letter came to us from the American friends. They had covenanted together, so they wrote, to remain at one in all things, and … had pledged themselves to make sacrifices in the pathway of the love of God, thus to achieve eternal life. At the very moment when this letter was read, together with the signatures at its close, 'Abdu'l-Bahá experienced a joy so vehement that no pen can describe it….[18]

An appreciation of the circumstances in which the expansion of the Cause in the West occurred is vital for present-day Bahá'ís, and for many reasons. It helps us abstract ourselves from the culture of coarse and intrusive communication that has become so commonplace in present-day society as to pass almost unnoticed. It draws to our attention the gentleness with which the Master chose to introduce to His Western audiences the concepts of human nature and human society revealed by Bahá'u'lláh, concepts revolutionary in their implications and entirely outside His hearers' experience. It explains the delicacy with which He used metaphors or relied on historical examples, the frequent indirectness of His approach, the intimacy He could summon up at will, and the apparently limitless patience with which He responded to questions, many of whose assumptions about reality had long since lost whatever validity they might once have possessed.

Yet another insight that a detached examination of the historical situation to which the Master addressed Himself in the West helps provide for our generation is an appreciation of the spiritual greatness of those who responded to Him. These souls answered His summons in spite, not because, of the liberal and economically advanced world they knew, a world they no doubt cherished and valued, and in which they had necessarily to carry on their daily lives. Their response arose from a level of consciousness that recognized, even if sometimes only dimly, the desperate need of the human race for spiritual enlightenment. To remain steadfast in their commitment to this insight required of these early believers—on whose sacrifice of self much of the foundation of the present-day Bahá'í communities both in the West and many other lands were laid—that they resist not only family and social pressures, but also the easy rationalizations of the world-view in which they had been raised and to which everything around them insistently exposed them. There was a heroism about the steadfastness of these early Western Bahá'ís that is, in its own way, as affecting as that of their Persian co-religionists who, in these same years, were facing persecution and death for the Faith they had embraced.

In the forefront of the Westerners who responded to the Master's summons were the little groups of intrepid believers whom Shoghi Effendi has hailed as "God-intoxicated pilgrims" and who had the privilege of visiting 'Abdu'l-Bahá in the prison-city of 'Akká, of seeing for themselves the luminosity of His Person and of hearing from His own lips words that had the power to transform human life. The effect on these believers has been expressed by May Maxwell:

"Of that first meeting," ... "I can remember neither joy nor pain, nor anything that I can name. I had been carried suddenly to too great a height, my soul had come in contact with the Divine Spirit, and this force, so pure, so holy, so mighty, had overwhelmed me...."[19]

Their return to their homes became, Shoghi Effendi explains, "the signal for an outburst of systematic and sustained activity, which ... spread its ramifications over Western Europe and the states and provinces of the North American continent...."[20] Fuelling their endeavours and those of their fellow believers, and drawing into the Cause growing numbers of new adherents, was a flood of Tablets addressed by the Master to recipients on both sides of the Atlantic, messages that threw open the imagination to the concepts, principles and ideals of God's new Revelation. The power of this creative force can be felt in the words with which the first American believer, Thornton Chase, sought to describe what he was seeing:

> His [the Master's] own writings, spreading like white-winged doves from the Center of His Presence to the ends of the earth, are so many (hundreds pouring forth daily) that it is an impossibility for him to have given time to them for searching thought or to have applied the mental processes of the scholar to them. They flow like streams from a gushing fountain....[21]

These sentiments add their own perspective to the determination with which the Master arose to undertake a venture so ambitious as to dismay many of those immediately around Him. Setting aside concerns expressed about His advanced age, His ill health, and the physical disabilities left by decades of imprisonment, He set out on a series of journeys that would last some three years, carrying Him eventually to the Pacific coast of the North American continent. The stresses and risks of international travel in the early years of the century were the least of the obstacles to the realization of the objectives He had set Himself. In the words of Shoghi Effendi:

> He Who, in His own words, had entered prison as a youth and left it an old man, Who never in His life had faced a public audience, had attended no school, had never moved in Western circles, and was unfamiliar with Western customs and language, had arisen not only to proclaim from pulpit and platform, in some of the chief capitals of

Europe and in the leading cities of the North American continent, the distinctive verities enshrined in His Father's Faith, but to demonstrate as well the Divine origin of the Prophets gone before Him, and to disclose the nature of the tie binding them to that Faith.[22]

No more brilliant a stage for the opening act of this great drama could have been desired than London, capital city of the largest and most cosmopolitan empire the world has ever known. In the eyes of the little groups of believers who had made the practical arrangements and who longed for the sight of His face, the trip was a triumph far surpassing their brightest hopes. Public officials, scholars, writers, editors, industrialists, leaders of reform movements, members of the British aristocracy, and influential clergymen of many denominations eagerly sought Him out, invited Him to their platforms, classrooms, homes and pulpits, and showered appreciation on the views He expounded. On Sunday, 10 September 1911, the Master spoke for the first time to a public audience anywhere, from the pulpit of the City Temple. His words evoked for His hearers the vision of a new age in the evolution of civilization:

> This is a new cycle of human power. All the horizons of the world are luminous, and the world will become indeed as a garden and a paradise.... You are loosed from ancient superstitions which have kept men ignorant, destroying the foundation of true humanity.

> The gift of God to this enlightened age is the knowledge of the oneness of mankind and of the fundamental oneness of religion. War shall cease between nations, and by the will of God the Most Great Peace shall come; the world will be seen as a new world, and all men will live as brothers.[23]

After an additional two months' stay in Paris and a return to Alexandria for a winter sojourn and the recuperation of His health, 'Abdu'l-Bahá sailed on 25 March 1912 to New York City, arriving on 11 April of that year. At even the simplest physical level, a programme packed with hundreds of public addresses, conferences and private talks in over forty cities across North America and an additional nineteen in Europe, some of them visited more than once, was a feat that may well have no parallel in modern history. On both continents, but especially in North America, 'Abdu'l-Bahá received a highly appreciative welcome from distinguished audiences devoted to such concerns as peace, women's rights, racial equality, social reform and moral development. On an almost daily basis, His talks and interviews received wide coverage in mass-circulation newspapers. He Himself was later to write that He had "observed all the doors open … and the ideal power of the Kingdom of God removing every obstacle and obstruction."[24]

The openness with which He was met permitted 'Abdu'l-Bahá to proclaim unambiguously the social principles of the new Revelation. Shoghi Effendi has summed up the truths thus presented:

> The independent search after truth, unfettered by superstition or tradition; the oneness of the entire human race, the pivotal principle and fundamental doctrine of the Faith; the basic unity of all religions; the condemnation of all forms of prejudice, whether religious, racial, class or national; the harmony which must exist between religion and science; the equality of men and women, the two wings on which the bird of human kind is able to soar; the introduction of compulsory education; the adoption of a universal auxiliary language; the abolition of the extremes of wealth and poverty; the institution of a world tribunal for the adjudication of disputes between nations; the exaltation of work, performed in the spirit of service, to the rank of worship; the glorification of justice as the ruling principle in human society, and of religion as a bulwark for the protection of all peoples and nations; and the establishment of a permanent and universal peace as the supreme goal of all mankind—these stand out as the essential elements of that Divine polity which He proclaimed to leaders of public thought as well as to the masses at large in the course of these missionary journeys.[25]

At the heart of the Master's message was the announcement that the long-promised Day for the unification of humanity and the establish-

ment on earth of the Kingdom of God had come. That Kingdom, as unveiled in 'Abdu'l-Bahá's letters and talks, owed nothing whatever to the
other-worldly assumptions familiar from the teachings of traditional
religion. Rather, the Master proclaimed the coming of age of humankind
and the emergence of a global civilization in which the development of
the whole range of human potentialities will be the fruit of the interaction between universal spiritual values, on the one hand, and, on the
other, material advances that were even then still undreamed of.

The means to achieve the goal, He said, had already come into existence. What was needed was the will to act and the faith to persist:

> All of us know that international peace is good, that it is the cause of
> life, but volition and action are necessary. Inasmuch as this century is
> the century of light, capacity for achieving peace has been assured. It
> is certain that these ideas will be spread among men to such a degree
> that they will result in action.[26]

Although expressed with unfailing courtesy and consideration, the
principles of the new Revelation were set out uncompromisingly in both
private and public encounters. Invariably, the Master's actions were as
eloquent as the words He used. In the United States, for example, nothing could have more clearly communicated Bahá'í belief in the oneness of
religion than 'Abdu'l-Bahá's readiness to include references to the Prophet
Muḥammad in addresses to Christian audiences and His energetic vindication of the divine origin of both Christianity and Islam to the
congregation at Temple Emanu-El in San Francisco. His ability to inspire
in women of all ages confidence that they possessed spiritual and intellectual capacities fully equal to those of men, His unprovocative but clear
demonstration of the meaning of Bahá'u'lláh's teachings on racial oneness
by welcoming black as well as white guests at His own dinner table and
the tables of His prominent hostesses, and His insistence on the overriding importance of unity in all aspects of Bahá'í endeavour—such
demonstrations of the way in which the spiritual and practical aspects of
life must interact threw open for the believers windows on a new world
of possibilities. The spirit of unconditional love in which these challenges
were phrased succeeded in overcoming the fears and uncertainties of

those whom the Master addressed.

Greater yet than the effort expended on His public exposition of the Cause was the time and energy the Master devoted to deepening the believers' understanding of the spiritual truths of Bahá'u'lláh's Revelation. In city after city, from early morning to late at night, the hours that were not taken up by the public demands of His mission were given over to responding to the questions of the friends, meeting their needs, and infusing into them a spirit of confidence in the contributions each could make to the promotion of the Cause they had embraced. His visit to Chicago provided the opportunity for 'Abdu'l-Bahá to lay, with His own hands, the cornerstone of the first Bahá'í House of Worship in the West, a project inspired by the one already under way in 'Ishqábád and likewise encouraged from the moment of its conception by 'Abdu'l-Bahá.

> The Mashriqu'l-Adhkár is one of the most vital institutions in the world, and it hath many subsidiary branches. Although it is a House of Worship, it is also connected with a hospital, a drug dispensary, a traveler's hospice, a school for orphans, and a university for advanced studies…. My hope is that the Mashriqu'l-Adhkár will now be established in America, and that gradually the hospital, the school, the university, the dispensary and the hospice, all functioning according to the most efficient and orderly procedures, will follow.[27]

As with the process simultaneously unfolding in Persia, only future historians will be able to appreciate adequately the creative power of this dimension of the Western trips. Memoirs and letters have testified to the way in which even brief encounters with the Master were to sustain countless Western Bahá'ís through the years of effort and sacrifice that followed, as they struggled to expand and consolidate the Faith. Without such an intervention by the Centre of the Covenant Himself, it is impossible to imagine little groups of Western believers—lacking entirely the spiritual heritage that their Persian co-religionists derived from the long involvement of parents and grandparents in the heroic events of Bábí and early Bahá'í history—being able so quickly to grasp what the Cause required of them and to undertake the daunting tasks involved.

His hearers were summoned to become the loving and confident agents of a great civilizing process, whose pivot is recognition of the oneness of the human race. In arising to undertake their mission, He promised that they would find unlocked in both themselves and others entirely new capacities with which God has in this Day endowed the human race:

> Ye must become the very soul of the world, the living spirit in the body of the children of men. In this wondrous Age, at this time when the Ancient Beauty, the Most Great Name, bearing unnumbered gifts, hath risen above the horizon of the world, the Word of God hath infused such awesome power into the inmost essence of humankind that He hath stripped men's human qualities of all effect, and hath, with His all-conquering might, unified the peoples in a vast sea of oneness.[28]

Nothing perhaps testifies so strikingly to the response the believers made to this appeal than the fact that the unity established among them did not inhibit their vivid individual ways of expressing the truths of the Faith. The relationship between the individual and the community has always been one of the most challenging issues in the development of society. One has only to read, even cursorily, accounts of the lives of the early Bahá'ís in the West to become aware of the high degree of individuality that characterized many of them, particularly the most active and creative. Not infrequently, they had found the Faith only after intensive investigation of various spiritual and social movements current at the time, and this broad understanding of the concerns and interests of their contemporaries no doubt helped make them such effective teachers of the Faith. It is equally clear, however, that the wide range of expression and understanding among them did not prevent them or their fellow believers from contributing to building a collective unity that was the chief attraction of the Cause. As the memoirs and historical accounts of the period make clear, the secret of this balancing of individual and community was the spiritual bond connecting all believers to the words and example of the Master. In an important sense 'Abdu'l-Bahá *was*, for all of them, the Bahá'í Cause.

No objective review of 'Abdu'l-Bahá's mission to the West can fail to take into account the sobering fact that only a small number of those who had accepted the Faith—and infinitely fewer among the public audiences who had thronged to hear His words—derived from these priceless opportunities more than a relatively dim understanding of the implications of His message. Appreciating these limitations on the part of His hearers, 'Abdu'l-Bahá did not hesitate to introduce into His relations with Western believers actions that summoned them to a level of consciousness far above mere social liberalism and tolerance. One example that must stand for a range of such interventions was His gentle but dramatic act in encouraging the marriage of Louis Gregory and Louise Mathew—the one black, the other white. The initiative set a standard for the American Bahá'í community as to the real meaning of racial integration, however timid and slow its members were in responding to the core implications of the challenge.

Even without a deep understanding of the Master's goals, those who embraced His message set out, often at great personal cost, to give practical expression to the principles He taught. Commitment to the cause of international peace; the abolition of extremes of wealth and poverty that were undermining the unity of society; the overcoming of national, racial and other prejudices; the encouragement of equality in the education of boys and girls; the need to shake off the shackles of ancient dogmas that were inhibiting investigation of reality—these principles for the advancement of civilization had made a powerful impression. What few, if any, of the Master's hearers grasped—perhaps could have grasped—was the revolutionary change in the very structure of society and the willing submission of human nature to Divine Law that, in the final analysis, can alone produce the necessary changes in attitude and behaviour.

The key to this vision of the coming transformation of the individual and social life of humankind was 'Abdu'l-Bahá's proclamation, shortly after His arrival in North America, of Bahá'u'lláh's Covenant

and of the central part He Himself had been called on to play in it. In
the Master's own words:

> As to the most great characteristic of the revelation of Bahá'u'lláh,
> a specific teaching not given by any of the Prophets of the past: It is
> the ordination and appointment of the Center of the Covenant. By
> this appointment and provision He has safeguarded and protected the
> religion of God against differences and schisms, making it impossible
> for anyone to create a new sect or faction of belief.[29]

Choosing New York City for His purpose—and designating it "the
City of the Covenant"—'Abdu'l-Bahá unveiled for Western believers the
devolution of authority made by the Founder of their Faith for the definitive interpretation of His Revelation. A highly regarded believer, Lua
Getsinger, had been called on by the Master to prepare the group of
Bahá'ís who had gathered in the house where He was temporarily residing for this historic announcement, following which He Himself went
downstairs and spoke in general terms about some of the implications
of the Covenant. Juliet Thompson, who, with one of the Persian trans-
lators, had been in the upstairs room at the time this mission had been
given to her friend, has left an account of the circumstances. She quotes
'Abdu'l-Bahá as saying:

> ...*I am the Covenant*, appointed by Bahá'u'lláh. And no one can
> refute His Word. This is the Testament of Bahá'u'lláh. You will find
> it in the Holy Book of Aqdas. Go forth and proclaim, "This is *the
> Covenant of God* in your midst."[30]

Conceived by Bahá'u'lláh as the Instrument which, in the words of
Shoghi Effendi, was "to perpetuate the influence of [the] Faith, insure
its integrity, safeguard it from schism, and stimulate its world-wide
expansion,"[31] the Covenant had been violated by members of
Bahá'u'lláh's own family almost immediately after His ascension. Recognizing that the authority invested in the Master by the Kitáb-i-'Ahd,
the Tablet of the Branch and related documents frustrated their private
hopes to turn the Cause to their personal advantage, these persons

began a persistent campaign to undermine His position, first in the
Holy Land and then in Persia, where the bulk of the Bahá'í community
was concentrated. When these schemes failed, they next sought to
manipulate the fears of the Ottoman government and the avarice of its
representatives in Palestine. This hope too collapsed when the "Young
Turk Revolution" overthrew the regime in Constantinople, hanging
some thirty-one of its leading officials, including several who had been
implicated in the plans of the Covenant-breakers.

In the West, during the early years of the Master's ministry, representatives sent by Him had already successfully countered the
machinations of Ibrahim Khayru'lláh—ironically, the individual who had
introduced many of the American believers to the Cause—who had
aimed at securing a position of leadership through association with the
Covenant-breakers in the Holy Family. Such experiences had doubtless
prepared the Western believers for the Master's formal proclamation of
His station and for the firmness with which He enjoined on believers
avoidance of any involvement with such agents of division: "Certain
weak, capricious, malicious and ignorant souls ... have striven to efface
the Divine Covenant and Testament, and render the clear water muddy
so that in it they might fish."[32] It would be only gradually, however, as the
new communities struggled to overcome differences of opinion and resist
the perennial human temptation to factionalism, that the implications of
this great organizing law of the new Dispensation would emerge.

While laying out in both public addresses and private discussions the
vision of a world of unity and peace that the Revelation of God for our
day will bring into being, the Master warned emphatically of the dangers
that lay on the immediate horizon—both for the Faith and for the world.
For both, 'Abdu'l-Bahá foresaw, in the words of Shoghi Effendi, a "winter of unprecedented severity".

For the Cause of God, that winter would entail heartbreaking betray-
als of the Covenant. In North America, the inconstancy of a small
number of individuals, frustrated in their aspirations for personal leadership, remained an ongoing source of difficulty for the community,
undermining the faith of some and causing others simply to drift away
from participation in the Faith. In Persia, too, the faith of the friends was

repeatedly tested by the schemes of ambitious individuals suddenly awakened to the possibilities for self-aggrandizement they believed they saw in
the successes attending the Master's work in the West. In both cases, the
consequences of such defections were ultimately to deepen the devotion
of the firm believers.

As for humanity in general, 'Abdu'l-Bahá warned in ominous terms
of the catastrophe that He saw approaching. While emphasizing the urgency of efforts at reconciliation that might alleviate in some measure
the suffering of the world's people, He left His hearers in no doubt of
the magnitude of the danger. In one of the major newspapers in
Montreal, where press coverage of the trip was particularly comprehensive, it was reported:

> "All Europe is an armed camp. These warlike preparations will
> necessarily culminate in a great war. The very armaments themselves
> are productive of war. This great arsenal must go ablaze. There is noth-
> ing of the nature of prophecy about such a view", said 'Abdu'l-Bahá;
> "it is based on reasoning solely."[33]

On 5 December 1912, the Figure who had been hailed across North
America as "the Apostle of Peace" sailed from New York for Liverpool.
After relatively brief stays in London and other British centres, He visited
several continental cities, again devoting several weeks to Paris, where He
had available the services of Hippolyte Dreyfus, whose written Arabic
and Persian met the Master's requirements. As the recognized cultural
capital of continental Europe, Paris was a focal centre for visitors from
many parts of the world, including the Orient. While the talks delivered
during His two extended visits to the city make frequent reference to the
great social issues discussed elsewhere, they seem particularly distinguished by an intimate spirituality that must have profoundly touched
the hearts of those privileged to meet Him:

> Lift up your hearts above the present and look with eyes of faith
> into the future! Today the seed is sown, the grain falls upon the
> earth, but behold the day will come when it shall rise a glorious tree
> and the branches thereof shall be laden with fruit. Rejoice and be

glad that this day has dawned, try to realize its power, for it is indeed wonderful![34]

On the morning of 13 June 1913, 'Abdu'l-Bahá embarked at Marseilles on the steamer *S. S. Himalaya,* arriving at Port Said in Egypt four days later. What Shoghi Effendi has called "His historic journeys" ended with His return to Haifa on 5 December 1913.

Two years, almost to the day, after 'Abdu'l-Bahá's statement to the editor of the *Montreal Daily Star,* the world that had enjoyed so intoxicating a sense of self-confidence and whose foundations had appeared impregnable, collapsed abruptly. The catastrophe is popularly associated with the murder in Sarajevo of the heir to the throne of the Austro-Hungarian empire, and certainly the train of blunders, reckless threats and mindless appeals to "honour" that led directly to World War I was ignited by this relatively minor event. In reality, however, as the Master had pointed out, preliminary "rumblings" during the entire first decade of the century should have alerted European leaders to the fragility of the existing order.

In the years 1904-1905, the Japanese and Russian empires had gone to war with a violence that led to the destruction of virtually the entire naval forces of the latter power and its surrender of territories it regarded as vital to its interests, a humiliation that was to have long-lasting domestic and international repercussions. On two occasions during these opening years of the century, war between France and Germany over imperialist designs in North Africa was narrowly averted only through the self-interested intervention of other powers. In 1911 Italian ambitions similarly provoked a dangerous threat to international peace by the seizure from the Ottoman empire of what is now Libya. International instability had been further deepened—as the Master had also warned—when Germany, feeling constrained by a growing web of hostile alliances, embarked on a massive naval building programme aimed at eliminating the previously accepted British lead.

Exacerbating these conflicts were tensions among the subject peoples of the Romanov, Hapsburg and Ottoman empires. Waiting only for some turn of events that would break the grip of the ramshackle systems that suppressed them, Balts, Poles, Czechs, Serbs, Greeks, Albanians, Bulgars, Romanians, Kurds, Arabs, Armenians, and a host of other nationalities looked forward eagerly to their day of liberation. Tirelessly exploiting this network of fissures in the existing order were a multitude of conspiracies, resistance groups and separatist organizations. Inspired by ideologies ranging from an almost incoherent anarchism at one extreme to sharply honed racist and nationalist obsessions at the other, these underground forces shared one naïve conviction: if the particular part of the prevailing order that had become their target could somehow be brought down, the inherent nobility of the segment of humankind that supported their aims—or the assumed nobility of humankind in general—would by itself ensure a new era of freedom and justice.

Alone among these would-be agents of violent change one broadly based movement was proceeding systematically and with ruthless clarity of purpose towards the goal of world revolution. The Communist Party, deriving both its intellectual thrust and an unshakeable confidence in its ultimate triumph from the writings of the nineteenth century ideologue Karl Marx, had succeeded in establishing groups of committed support-ers throughout Europe and various other countries. Convinced that the genius of its master had demonstrated beyond question the essentially material nature of the forces that had given rise to both human con-sciousness and social organization, the Communist movement dismissed the validity of both religion and "bourgeois" moral standards. In its view, faith in God was a neurotic weakness indulged in by the human race, a weakness that had merely permitted successive ruling classes to manipu-late superstition as an instrument for enslaving the masses.

To the leaders of the world, blindly edging their way towards the uni-versal conflagration which pride and folly had prepared, the great strides being made by science and technology represented chiefly a means of gaining military advantage over their rivals. The European opponents of the nations concerned, however, were not the poverty-stricken and largely uneducated colonial populations whom they had been able to subject. The false confidence that military hardware thus inspired led inexorably to a race to equip armies and navies with the most advanced of modern weaponry, and to do so on as massive a scale as possible. Machine guns, long-range cannon, "dreadnoughts", submarines, landmines, poison gas and the possibility of equipping airplanes for bombing attacks emerged as features of what one commentator has termed the "technology of death".[35] All of these instruments of annihilation would, as 'Abdu'l-Bahá had warned, be deployed and refined during the course of the coming conflict.

Science and technology were also exerting other, more subtle pressures on the prevailing order. Large-scale industrial production, fuelled by the arms race, had accelerated the movement of populations into urban centres. By the end of the preceding century, this process was already undermining inherited standards and loyalties, exposing growing numbers of people to novel ideas for the bringing about of social change, and exciting mass appetites for material benefits previously available only to elite segments of society. Even under relatively autocratic systems, the public was beginning to perceive the extent to which civil authority was dependent for its effectiveness on its ability to win broad popular support. These social developments would have unforeseen and far-reaching consequences. As war would drag endlessly on and unthinking faith in its simplicities come into question, millions of men in conscript armies on both sides would begin to see their sufferings as meaningless in themselves and fruitless in terms of their own and their families' well-being.

Beyond these implications of technological and economic change, scientific advancement seemed to encourage easy assumptions about human nature, the almost unnoticed overlay that Bahá'u'lláh has termed "the obscuring dust of all acquired knowledge".[36] These unexamined views communicated themselves to ever-widening audiences. Sensationalism in the popular press, fiery debates between scientists or scholars, on the one hand, and theologians or influential clergymen, on the other, along with the rapid spread of public education, continued to undermine the authority of accepted religious doctrines, as well as of prevailing moral standards.

These seismic forces of the new century combined to make the situation facing the Western world in 1914 intensely volatile. When the great conflagration did break out, therefore, the nightmare far surpassed the worst fears of thoughtful minds. It would serve no purpose here to review the exhaustively analyzed cataclysm of World War I. The statistics themselves remain almost beyond the ability of the human mind to encompass: an estimated sixty million men eventually being thrown into the most horrific inferno that history had ever known, eight million of them perishing in the course of the war and an additional ten million or more being permanently disabled by crippling injuries, burned-out lungs and appalling disfigurements.[37] Historians have suggested that the total financial cost may have reached thirty billion dollars, wiping out a substantial portion of the total capital wealth of Europe.

Even such massive losses do not begin to suggest the full scope of the ruin. One of the considerations that long held back President Woodrow Wilson from proposing to the United States Congress the declaration of war that had by then become virtually inescapable was his awareness of the moral damage that would ensue. Not the least of the distinctions that characterized this extraordinary man—a statesman whose vision both 'Abdu'l-Bahá and Shoghi Effendi have praised—was his understanding of the brutalization of human nature that would be the worst legacy of the tragedy that was by then engulfing Europe, a legacy beyond human capacity to reverse.[38]

Reflection on the magnitude of the suffering experienced by humankind in the war's four years—and the resulting setback to the long, painful process of the civilizing of human nature—lends tragic force to words the Master had addressed only two or three years earlier to audiences in such European cities as London, Paris, Vienna, Budapest and Stuttgart, as well as in North America. Speaking one evening in the home of Mr. and Mrs. Sutherland Maxwell in Montreal, He had said:

> Today the world of humanity is walking in darkness because it is out of touch with the world of God. That is why we do not see the signs of God in the hearts of men. The power of the Holy Spirit has no influence. When a divine spiritual illumination becomes manifest

in the world of humanity, when divine instruction and guidance appear, then enlightenment follows, a new spirit is realized within, a new power descends, and a new life is given. It is like the birth from the animal kingdom into the kingdom of man.... I will pray, and you must pray, likewise, that such heavenly bounty may be realized; that strife and enmity may be banished, warfare and bloodshed taken away; that hearts may attain ideal communication and that all people may drink from the same fountain.[39]

The vindictive peace treaty, imposed by the Allied powers on their defeated enemies, succeeded only, as both 'Abdu'l-Bahá and Shoghi Effendi have pointed out, in planting the seeds of another, far more terrible conflict. The ruinous reparations demanded of the vanquished —and the injustice that required them to accept the full guilt for a war for which all parties had been, to one degree or another, responsible— were among the factors that would prepare demoralized peoples in Europe to embrace totalitarian promises of relief which they might not otherwise have contemplated.

Ironically, no matter how harsh were the reparations required of the defeated, the supposed victors awoke to the appalled realization that their triumph—and the demand for unconditional surrender that had driven it—had come at an equally crippling price. Staggering war debts ended forever the economic dominance which these European nations had acquired through three centuries of imperialist exploitation of the rest of the planet. The deaths of millions of young men who would have been urgently needed to meet the challenges of the coming decades was a loss that could never be recovered. Indeed, Europe itself—which only four brief years earlier had represented the apparent summit of civilization and world influence—lost at one stroke this pre-eminence, and began the inexorable slide during the following decades toward the status of an auxiliary to a rising new centre of power in North America.

Initially, it seemed that the vision of the future conceived by Woodrow Wilson would now be realized. In part, this proved to be the case as subject peoples throughout Europe gained the freedom to work out their own destinies through the emergence from the ruin of the former empires of a series of new nation-states. Further, the president's "Fourteen Points" briefly endowed his public statements with so great a moral authority in the minds of millions of Europeans that not even the most recalcitrant of his fellow leaders among the Allied powers could entirely disregard his wishes. Despite months of wrangling over colonies, borders, and clauses in the text of the peace treaty, the Versailles settlement eventually incorporated an attenuated form of the proposed League of Nations, an institution which it was hoped could adjust future disputes between nations and harmonize international affairs.

Shoghi Effendi's commentary on the significance of this historic initiative commands reflection on the part of every Bahá'í who seeks to understand the events of this turbulent century. Describing two closely interrelated developments that are associated with the dawn of world peace, he lays emphasis on the fact that they are "destined to culminate, in the fullness of time, in a single glorious consummation".[40] The first, the Guardian describes as associated with the mission of the Bahá'í community in the North American continent; the second, with the destiny of the United States as a nation. Speaking of this latter phenomenon, which dated back to the outbreak of the first world war, Shoghi Effendi writes:

> It received its initial impetus through the formulation of President Wilson's Fourteen Points, closely associating for the first time that republic with the fortunes of the Old World. It suffered its first setback through the dissociation of that republic from the newly born League of Nations which that president had labored to create.... It must, however long and tortuous the way, lead, through a series of victories and reverses, to the political unification of the Eastern and Western Hemispheres, to the emergence of a world government and the establishment of the Lesser Peace, as foretold by Bahá'u'lláh and foreshadowed by the Prophet Isaiah. It must, in the end, culminate in the unfurling of the banner of the Most Great Peace, in the Golden Age of the Dispensation of Bahá'u'lláh.[41]

How tragic, therefore, was the fate of the conception that had inspired the efforts of the American president. As soon became apparent, the League had been stillborn. Although it included such features as a legislature, a judiciary, an executive, and a supporting bureaucracy, it had been denied the authority vital to the work it was ostensibly intended to perform. Locked into the nineteenth century's conception of untrammelled national sovereignty, it could take decisions only with the unanimous assent of the member states, a requirement largely ruling out effective action.[42] The hollowness of the system was exposed, as well, by its failure to include some of the world's most powerful states: Germany had been rejected as a defeated nation held responsible for the war, Russia was initially denied entrance because of its Bolshevik regime, and the United States itself refused—as a result of narrow political partisanship in Congress—either to join the League or to ratify the treaty. Ironically, even the half-hearted efforts made to protect ethnic minorities living in the newly created nation-states proved eventually to be little more than weapons to be used in Europe's continuing fratricidal conflicts.

In sum, at precisely the moment in human history when an unprecedented outbreak of violence had undermined the inherited bulwarks of civilized behaviour, the political leadership of the Western world had emasculated the one alternative system of international order to which experience of this catastrophe had given birth and which alone could have alleviated the far greater suffering that lay ahead. In the prophetic words of 'Abdu'l-Bahá: "Peace, Peace ... the lips of potentates and peoples unceasingly proclaim, whereas the fire of unquenched hatreds still smoulders in their hearts." "The ills from which the world now suffers," He added in 1920, "will multiply; the gloom which envelops it will deepen.... The vanquished Powers will continue to agitate. They will resort to every measure that may rekindle the flame of war."[43]

As war's inferno was engulfing the world, 'Abdu'l-Bahá turned His attention to the one great task remaining in His ministry, that of ensuring the proclamation to the remotest corners of the Earth of the message which had been neglected—or opposed—in Islamic and Western society alike. The instrument He devised for this purpose was the Divine Plan laid out in fourteen great Tablets, four of them addressed to the Bahá'í community of North America and ten subsidiary ones addressed to five specific segments of that community. Together with Bahá'u'lláh's Tablet of Carmel and the Master's Will and Testament, the Tablets of the Divine Plan were described by Shoghi Effendi as three of the "Charters" of the Cause. Revealed during the darkest days of the war, in 1916 and 1917, the Divine Plan summoned the small body of American and Canadian believers to assume the role of leadership in establishing the Cause of God throughout the planet. The implications of the trust were awe-inspiring. In the words of the Master:

> The hope which 'Abdu'l-Bahá cherishes for you is that the same success which has attended your efforts in America may crown your endeavors in other parts of the world, that through you the fame of the Cause of God may be diffused throughout the East and the West, and the advent of the Kingdom of the Lord of Hosts be proclaimed in all the five continents of the globe. The moment this Divine Message is carried forward by the American believers from the shores of America, and is propagated through the continents of Europe, of Asia, of Africa and of Australia, and as far as the islands of the Pacific, this community will find itself securely established upon the throne of an everlasting dominion. Then will all the peoples of the world witness that this community is spiritually illumined and divinely guided. Then will the whole earth resound with the praises of its majesty and greatness....[44]

Shoghi Effendi reminds us that this historic mission, described by him as "the birthright of the North American Bahá'í Community",[45] is rooted in the words of the Twin Manifestations of God to humanity's age of maturity. It appeared first in the words of the Báb, who called on the "peoples of the West" to "issue forth from your cities", to "aid God ere the Day when the Lord of mercy shall come down unto you in the shadow of the clouds...", and to become "as true brethren in the one and indivisible religion of God, free from distinction,... so that ye find yourselves reflected in them, and they in you".[46] In His summons to the "Rulers of America and the Presidents of the Republics therein", Bahá'u'lláh Himself delivered a mandate that has no parallel in any of His other addresses to world leaders: "Bind ye the broken with the hands of justice, and crush the oppressor who flourisheth with the rod of the commandments of your Lord, the Ordainer, the All-Wise."[47] It was Bahá'u'lláh, too, who enunciated one of the most profound truths about the process by which civilization has evolved: "In the East the light of His Revelation hath broken; in the West have appeared the signs of His dominion. Ponder this in your hearts, O people...."[48]

Although the Divine Plan would, as the Guardian was later to say, "be held in abeyance" until the system necessary to its execution had been brought into being, 'Abdu'l-Bahá had selected, empowered and mandated a company of believers who would take the lead in launching the enterprise. His own life was now swiftly moving to its end, but the three years left to Him after the conclusion of the world war seemed, in retrospect, to provide a foretaste of the victories that the Cause itself would know as the century unfolded. The changed conditions in the Holy Land freed the Master to pursue His work unhampered and created the conditions in which the brilliance of His mind and spirit could exercise their influence on government officials, visiting dignitaries of every kind, and the various communities making up the population of the Holy Land. The Mandate Power itself sought to express its appreciation of the unifying effect of His example and the philanthropic work He did by conferring on Him a knighthood.[49] More importantly, a renewed flow of pilgrims and of Tablets to Bahá'í communities of both East and West stimulated an expansion in the teaching work and a deepening of the friends' understanding of the implications of the Faith's message.

Nothing perhaps illustrated so dramatically the spiritual triumph the Master had won at the World Centre of the Faith than the events in Haifa that occurred immediately after His ascension in the early hours of 28 November 1921. The following day a vast concourse of thousands of people, representing the variegated races and sects of the region, followed the funeral cortège up the slopes of Mount Carmel in a state of unaffected grief such as the city had never before witnessed. It was led by representatives of the British government, members of the diplomatic community, and the heads of all of the religious bodies in the area, several of whom participated in the service at the Shrine of the Báb. So unrestrained and unified an outburst of mourning reflected a sudden awareness of the loss of a Figure whose example had served as a focal centre of unity in an angry and divided land. In itself, it served for all with eyes to see as a compelling vindication of the truth of the oneness of humankind which the Master had tirelessly proclaimed.

IV

WITH THE PASSING OF 'ABDU'L-BAHÁ, the Apostolic Age of the Cause reached its end. The Divine intervention that had begun seventy-seven years earlier on the night the Báb declared His mission to Mulla Ḥusayn—and 'Abdu'l-Bahá Himself was born—had completed its work. It had been, in the words of Shoghi Effendi, "a period whose splendours no victories in this or any future age, however brilliant, can rival...."[50] Ahead lay the thousand or thousands of years in which the potentialities that this creative force has planted in human consciousness will gradually unfold.

Contemplation of so great a juncture in the history of civilization brings into sharp focus the Figure whose nature and role have been unique in this six-thousand-year process. Bahá'u'lláh has called 'Abdu'l-Bahá "the Mystery of God". Shoghi Effendi has described Him as "the Centre and Pivot" of Bahá'u'lláh's Covenant, the "perfect Exemplar" of the teachings of the Revelation of God for the age of human maturity, and "the Mainspring of the Oneness of Humanity". No phenomenon in any way comparable to His appearance had accompanied any of the Divine Revelations that had given birth to the other great religious systems in recorded history; all of these had been essentially stages preparing humanity for its coming of age. 'Abdu'l-Bahá was Bahá'u'lláh's supreme Creation, the One that made

everything else possible. An understanding of this truth moved a perceptive American Bahá'í to write:

> Now a message from God must be delivered, and there was no
> mankind to hear this message. Therefore, God gave the world
> 'Abdu'l-Bahá. 'Abdu'l-Bahá received the message of Bahá'u'lláh on
> behalf of the human race. He heard the voice of God; He was in-
> spired by the spirit; He attained complete consciousness and
> awareness of the meaning of this message, and He pledged the human
> race to respond to the voice of God. ...to me *that* is the Covenant—
> that there was on this earth some one who could be a representative of
> an as yet uncreated race. There were only tribes, families, creeds, classes,
> etc., but there was no man except 'Abdu'l-Bahá, and 'Abdu'l-Bahá, as
> man, took to Himself the message of Bahá'u'lláh and promised God
> that He would bring the people into the *oneness of mankind*, and create
> a humanity that could be the vehicle for the laws of God.[51]

Beginning His mission as a prisoner of a brutal, ignorant regime and
relentlessly assailed by faithless brothers who ultimately sought His
death, the Master single-handedly created of the Persian Bahá'í community a brilliant demonstration of the social development the Cause
could produce, inspired the expansion of the Faith across the Orient,
raised up communities of devoted believers throughout the West,
designed a Plan for the world-wide expansion of the Cause, won the respect and admiration of leaders of thought wherever His influence
reached, and provided Bahá'u'lláh's followers throughout the world
with a vast body of authoritative guidance as to the intent of the Faith's
laws and teachings. On the slopes of Mount Carmel He erected with
enormous pain and difficulty the Shrine housing the mortal remains of
the martyred Báb, the focal point of the processes by which the life of
our planet will gradually be organized. Through it all, in every least
occasion of a life filled with cares and demands of every sort—a life
exposed at all times to examination by enemy and friend alike—He ensured that posterity will possess that treasure of which poets,
philosophers and mystics have dreamed all down the ages, a demonstration of unshadowed human perfection.

And finally, it was 'Abdu'l-Bahá who made certain that the Divine Order conceived by Bahá'u'lláh for the unification of the human race and the institution of justice in humanity's collective life would be provided with the means required to realize its Founder's purpose. For unity to exist among human beings—at even the simplest level—two fundamental conditions must pertain. Those involved must first of all be in some agreement about the nature of reality as it affects their relationships with one another and with the phenomenal world. They must, secondly, give assent to some recognized and authoritative means by which decisions will be taken that affect their association with one another and that determine their collective goals.

Unity is not, that is, merely a condition resulting from a sense of mutual goodwill and common purpose, however profound and sincerely held such sentiments may be, any more than an organism is a product of some fortuitous and amorphous association of various elements. Unity is a phenomenon of creative power, whose existence becomes apparent through the effects that collective action produces and whose absence is betrayed by the impotence of such efforts. However handicapped it often has been by ignorance and perversity, this force has been the primary influence driving the advancement of civilization, generating legal codes, social and political institutions, artistic works, technological achievements without end, moral breakthroughs, material prosperity, and long periods of public peace whose afterglow lived in the memories of subsequent generations as imagined "golden ages".

Through the Revelation of God to humanity's coming of age, the full potentialities of this creative force have at last been released and the means necessary to the realization of the Divine purpose have been instituted. In His Will and Testament, which Shoghi Effendi has described as the "Charter" of the Administrative Order, 'Abdu'l-Bahá set out in detail the nature and role of the twin institutions that are His appointed Successors and whose complementary functions ensure the unity of the Bahá'í Cause and the achievement of its mission throughout the Dispensation, the Guardianship and the Universal House of Justice. He laid particularly strong emphasis on the authority thus conveyed:

Whatsoever they decide is of God. Whoso obeyeth him not, neither obeyeth them, hath not obeyed God; whoso rebelleth against
him and against them hath rebelled against God; whoso opposeth
him hath opposed God; whoso contendeth with them hath con-
tended with God....[52]

Shoghi Effendi has explained the significance of this extraordinary Text:

The Administrative Order which this historic Document has established, it should be noted, is, by virtue of its origin and character,
unique in the annals of the world's religious systems. No Prophet before Bahá'u'lláh, it can be confidently asserted,... has established,
authoritatively and in writing, anything comparable to the Administrative Order which the authorized Interpreter of Bahá'u'lláh's
teachings has instituted, an Order which ... must and will, in a manner unparalleled in any previous religion, safeguard from schism the
Faith from which it has sprung.[53]

Before the reading and promulgation of the Will and Testament, the
great majority of the members of the Faith had assumed that the next stage
in the evolution of the Cause would be the election of the Universal House
of Justice, the institution founded by Bahá'u'lláh Himself in the Kitáb-i-
Aqdas as the governing body of the Bahá'í world. An important fact for
present-day Bahá'ís to understand is that prior to this point the concept of
Guardianship was unknown to the Bahá'í community. There was widespread rejoicing at the news of the unique distinction that the Master had
conferred on Shoghi Effendi and the continuing link with the Founders of
the Faith that his role represented. Until then, however, there had been no
appreciation of Bahá'u'lláh's intent that such an institution should emerge
or of the interpretive function it would have to perform—a function whose
vital importance has since become readily apparent and which hindsight
makes clear was implicit in certain of His Writings.

What was entirely beyond the imagination of anyone then living,
whether faithful or ill-disposed, was the transformation in the life of the
Cause that the Will of the Master set in motion. "Were ye to know what
will come to pass after Me," 'Abdu'l-Bahá had declared, "surely would ye
pray that my end be hastened."[54]

V

AN APPRECIATION OF THE PLACE of the Guardianship in Bahá'í history must begin with an objective consideration of the circumstances in which Shoghi Effendi's mission had to be carried out. Particularly important is the fact that the first half of this ministry unfolded between wars, a period marked by deepening uncertainty and anxiety about all aspects of human affairs. On the one hand, significant advances had been made in overcoming barriers between nations and classes; on the other, political impotence and a resulting economic paralysis greatly handicapped efforts to take advantage of these openings. There was everywhere a sense that some fundamental redefinition of the nature of society and the role its institutions should play was urgently needed—a redefinition, indeed, of the purpose of human life itself.

In important respects, humanity found itself at the end of the first world war able to explore possibilities never before imagined. Throughout Europe and the Near East the absolutist systems that had been among the most powerful barriers to unity had been swept away. To a great extent, too, fossilized religious dogmas that had lent moral endorsement to the forces of conflict and alienation were everywhere in question. Former subject peoples were free to consider plans for their collective

futures and to assume responsibility for their relationships with one another through the instrumentality of the new nation-states created by the
Versailles settlement. The same ingenuity that had gone into producing
weapons of destruction was being turned to the challenging, but reward-
ing, tasks of economic expansion. Out of the darkest days of the war had
come poignant stories, such as the impulse that had briefly moved British and German soldiers to leave the slaughterhouse of the trenches to
commemorate together the birth of Christ, providing a flickering glimpse
of the oneness of the human race which the Master had tirelessly proclaimed in His journeys across that same continent. Most important of
all, an extraordinary effort of imagination had brought the unification of
humanity one immense step forward. The world's leaders, however reluc-
tantly, had created an international consultative system which, though
crippled by vested interests, gave the ideal of international order its first
suggestion of shape and structure.

The post-war awakening expressed itself world-wide. Under the leadership of Sun Yat-sen, the Chinese people had already thrown off the
decadent imperial regime that had compromised the country's well-
being, and were seeking to lay foundations of a rebirth of that country's
greatness. Throughout Latin America, despite terrible and repeated setbacks, popular movements were likewise struggling to gain control over
their countries' destinies and the use of their continent's immense natural resources. In India, one of the century's most remarkable figures,
Mohandas Gandhi, embarked on an enterprise that would not only revo-
lutionize the fortunes of his country, but also demonstrate conclusively to
the world what spiritual force can achieve. Africa was still awaiting its
moment of destiny, as were the inhabitants of other colonial lands, but
for anyone with eyes to see, a process of change had been set in motion
that could ultimately not be suppressed, because it represented the universal yearnings of humankind.

These advances, however encouraging, could not conceal the historic
tragedy that had occurred. During the second half of the nineteenth
century, the proclamation of the Day of God addressed by Bahá'u'lláh
to the rulers of His day, in whose hands lay the destiny of humankind,
had been either rejected or ignored by its recipients in both East and

West. Reflection on so great a breach of faith throws into sobering perspective the subsequent response that had met the mission of
'Abdu'l-Bahá to the West. However much one may rejoice in the praise
poured on the Master from every quarter, the immediate results of His
efforts represented yet another immense moral failure on the part of a
considerable portion of humankind and of its leadership. The message
that had been suppressed in the East was essentially ignored by a Western
world which had proceeded down the path of ruin long prepared for it by
overweening self-satisfaction, leading finally to the betrayal of the ideal
embodied in the League of Nations.

In consequence, the two decades immediately after Shoghi Effendi
assumed his responsibility for the vindication of the Cause of God were
a period of deepening gloom throughout the Western world, which
seemed to reflect a massive setback in the process of integration and enlightenment so confidently proclaimed by the Master. It was as if
political, social and economic life had fallen into a kind of limbo. Grave
doubts developed about the capacity of the liberal democratic tradition to
cope with the problems of the times; indeed, in a number of European
countries, governments inspired by such principles were replaced by
authoritarian regimes. Soon, the economic crash of 1929 led to a world-
wide reduction in material well-being, with all the further moral and
psychological insecurities that resulted.

An appreciation of these circumstances helps us to understand the
magnitude of the challenge facing Shoghi Effendi at the outset of his
ministry. So far as the objective condition of humankind, as he encountered it, was concerned, there was nothing that would have inspired
confidence that the vision of a new world bequeathed him by the Founders of the Bahá'í Cause could be significantly advanced during whatever
span of years might be allowed him.

Nor did the instrument available to him appear to possess the strength,
the resilience or the sophistication his task required. In 1923, when Shoghi
Effendi was eventually able to assume full direction of the Cause, the core
of Bahá'u'lláh's followers consisted of the body of believers in Iran, of
whose number not even a reliable estimate could have then been produced.
Denied most of the means necessary to their promotion of the Cause, and

severely limited in the material resources at their disposal, the Iranian community was hedged about by constant harassment. In North America, charged with the daunting responsibilities of the Divine Plan, small communities of believers found themselves struggling with the simple challenges of making a livelihood for themselves and their families as the economic crisis steadily deepened. In Europe, Australasia and the Far East, even smaller Bahá'í groups kept the flame of the Faith alive, as did isolated groups, families and individuals scattered throughout the rest of the world. Literature, even in English, was inadequate, and the task of translating the Writings into other major languages and of finding the funds to publish them represented an almost impossible burden.

Though the vision communicated by the Master burned as brightly as ever, the means at their disposal must have appeared to Bahá'ís as pitifully inadequate in the face of the conditions prevailing everywhere. The hulking black foundation of the future Mother Temple of the West, rising over the lake front north of Chicago, seemed to mock the brilliant conception that had dazzled the architectural world only a few years before. In Baghdad, the "Most Holy House", designated by Bahá'u'lláh as the focal centre of Bahá'í pilgrimage, had been seized by opponents of the Faith. In the Holy Land itself, the Mansion of Bahá'u'lláh was falling into ruin as a result of neglect by the Covenant-breakers who occupied it, and the Shrine housing the precious remains of both the Báb and 'Abdu'l-Bahá had progressed no further than the simple stone structure raised by the Master.

A series of exploratory consultations with leading Bahá'ís made it clear to the Guardian that even a formal discussion with qualified believers about the creation of an international secretariat would be not only useless, but probably counterproductive. It was alone, therefore, that Shoghi Effendi set out on the task of propelling forward the vast enterprise entrusted to his hands. How completely alone he was is almost impossible for the present generation of Bahá'ís to grasp; to the extent one does grasp it, the realization is acutely painful.

Initially, the Guardian assumed that the members of the Master's extended family, whose distinguished lineage brought them immense respect from Bahá'ís everywhere, would welcome the opportunity to assist him in realizing the purpose that the Master's Will had set out in language so imperative and moving. Accordingly, he invited his brothers, his cousins and one of his sisters, whose education made them qualified for the purpose, to provide the administrative support that the demanding work of the Guardianship required. Tragically, as time passed, one after another of these persons proved dissatisfied with the supporting role thus assigned and careless in the discharge of its functions. Far more seriously, Shoghi Effendi found himself facing a situation in which the authority conferred on him, although expressed in uncompromising terms in the Will and Testament, was seen by those related to him as relatively nominal in character. These individuals preferred to regard the leadership of the Faith as essentially a family affair in which great weight should be placed on the views of senior figures among them, who were supposedly qualified to assume such a prerogative. Beginning with demonstrations of sullen resistance, the situation steadily deteriorated to a point where the children and grandchildren of 'Abdu'l-Bahá felt free to disagree with His appointed successor and to disobey his instructions.

Rúhíyyih Khánum, who saw this process of deterioration in its later stages and herself suffered greatly in witnessing its effects on both the work of the Cause and the Guardian personally, has written:

> …one must understand the old story of Cain and Abel, the story of family jealousies which, like a sombre thread in the fabric of history, runs through all its epochs and can be traced in all its events…. The weakness of the human heart, which so often attaches itself to an unworthy object, the weakness of the human mind, prone to conceit and self-assurance in personal opinions, involve people in a welter of emotions that blind their judgment and lead them far astray…. Even though this phenomenon of Covenant-breaking seems to be an inherent aspect of religion this does not mean it produces no damaging effect on the Cause…. Above all it does not mean that a devastating effect is not produced on the Centre of the Covenant himself. Shoghi Effendi's whole life was darkened by the vicious personal attacks made upon him.[55]

This sombre background casts in an all the more brilliant light the achievements of the Greatest Holy Leaf, sister of 'Abdu'l-Bahá and last survivor of the Faith's Heroic Age. Bahíyyih Khánum played a vital role in guarding the interests of the Cause after the Master's death and became Shoghi Effendi's sole effective support. Her fidelity evoked from his pen perhaps the most deeply moving passages he was ever to write. The apostrophe he addressed to her after her passing in 1932 was set in a letter to the Bahá'ís "throughout the West", which itself read in part:

> Only future generations and pens abler than mine can, and will, pay a worthy tribute to the towering grandeur of her spiritual life, to the unique part she played throughout the tumultuous stages of Bahá'í history, to the expressions of unqualified praise that have streamed from the pen of both Bahá'u'lláh and 'Abdu'l-Bahá, the Center of His covenant, though unrecorded, and in the main unsuspected by the mass of her passionate admirers in East and West, the share she has had in influencing the course of some of the chief events in the annals of the Faith, the sufferings she bore, the sacrifices she made, the rare gifts of unfailing sympathy she so strikingly displayed—these, and many others stand so inextricably interwoven with the fabric of the Cause itself that no future historian of the Faith of Bahá'u'lláh can afford to ignore or minimize....Which of the blessings am I to recount, which in her unfailing solicitude she showered upon me, in the most critical and agitated hours of my life? To me, standing in so dire a need of the vitalizing grace of God, she was the living symbol of many an attribute I had learned to admire in 'Abdu'l-Bahá.[56]

For long years, the Guardian felt that the protection of the Cause required him to maintain silence about the deteriorating situation in the Holy Family. Only as opposition finally burst into acts of open defiance, eventually involving the family in shameful collaboration and even marriages with members of the very band of Covenant-breakers against whose treachery the Will and Testament of the Master had warned in vehement language, as well as with a local family deeply hostile to the Cause, did Shoghi Effendi eventually feel compelled to expose to the Bahá'í world the nature of the delinquencies with which he was having to deal.[57]

This sad history is of importance to an understanding of the Cause in the twentieth century not only because of what the Guardian called the "havoc" it wreaked in the Holy Family, but because of the light it casts on the challenges the Bahá'í community will increasingly face in the years ahead, challenges predicted in explicit language by both the Master and the Guardian. Apart from the insincerity that marked all too many of them, the relatives of Shoghi Effendi demonstrated little or no awareness of the spiritual nature of the role conferred on him in the Will and Testament. That the Revelation of God to the age of humanity's maturity should have brought with it, as a central feature of its mission, an authority essential for the restructuring of social order represented a spiritual challenge they seemed unable, or perhaps never sought, to understand. Their abandonment of the Guardian is a lesson that will remain with posterity down through the centuries of the Bahá'í Dispensation. The fate of this most privileged but unworthy company of human beings underlines for all who read their story both the significance that the Covenant of Bahá'u'lláh holds for the unification of humankind and the uncompromising demands it makes on those who seek its shelter.

In considering the events of the ministry of Shoghi Effendi, Bahá'ís need to make the effort of imagination to see, through his eyes, the nature of the mission laid on him. Our guide is the body of writings he has left. 'Abdu'l-Bahá had proclaimed in countless Tablets and talks the pivotal principle of Bahá'u'lláh's message: "In this wondrous Revelation, this glorious century, the foundation of the Faith of God and the distinguishing feature of His Law is the consciousness of the Oneness of Mankind."[58] 'Abdu'l-Bahá had been equally emphatic in asserting, as already noted, that the revolutionary changes taking place in every field of human endeavour now made the unification of humanity a realistic objective. It was this vision that, for the thirty-six years of his Guardianship, provided the organizing force of Shoghi Effendi's work. Its implications were the theme of some of the most important messages he wrote.

Addressing in 1931 the friends in the West, he opened for them a brilliant vista:

> The principle of the Oneness of Mankind—the pivot round which all the teachings of Bahá'u'lláh revolve—is no mere outburst of ignorant emotionalism or an expression of vague and pious hope. Its appeal is not to be merely identified with a reawakening of the spirit of brotherhood and good-will among men, nor does it aim solely at the fostering of harmonious coöperation among individual peoples and nations. Its implications are deeper, its claims greater than any which the Prophets of old were allowed to advance. Its message is applicable not only to the individual, but concerns itself primarily with the nature of those essential relationships that must bind all the states and nations as members of one human family.... It implies an organic change in the structure of present-day society, a change such as the world has not experienced.... It calls for no less than the reconstruction and the demilitarization of the whole civilized world —a world organically unified in all the essential aspects of its life, its political machinery, its spiritual aspiration, its trade and finance, its script and language, and yet infinite in the diversity of the national characteristics of its federated units.[59]

A concept that showed itself strongly in the Guardian's writings was the organic metaphor in which Bahá'u'lláh, and subsequently 'Abdu'l-Bahá, had captured the millennia-long process that has carried humanity to this culminating point in its collective history. That image was the analogy that can be drawn between, on the one hand, the stages by which human society has been gradually organized and integrated, and, on the other, the process by which each human being slowly develops out of the limitations of infantile existence into the powers of maturity. It appears prominently in several of Shoghi Effendi's writings on the transformation taking place in our time:

> The long ages of infancy and childhood, through which the human race had to pass, have receded into the background. Humanity is now experiencing the commotions invariably associated with the

most turbulent stage of its evolution, the stage of adolescence, when the impetuosity of youth and its vehemence reach their climax, and must gradually be superseded by the calmness, the wisdom, and the maturity that characterize the stage of manhood.[60]

Deliberation on this vast conception was to lead Shoghi Effendi to provide the Bahá'í world with a coherent description of the future that has since permitted three generations of believers to articulate for governments, media and the general public in every part of the world the perspective in which the Bahá'í Faith pursues its work:

> The unity of the human race, as envisaged by Bahá'u'lláh, implies the establishment of a world commonwealth in which all nations, races, creeds and classes are closely and permanently united, and in which the autonomy of its state members and the personal freedom and initiative of the individuals that compose them are definitely and completely safeguarded. This commonwealth must, as far as we can visualize it, consist of a world legislature, whose members will, as the trustees of the whole of mankind, ultimately control the entire resources of all the component nations, and will enact such laws as shall be required to regulate the life, satisfy the needs and adjust the relationships of all races and peoples. A world executive, backed by an international Force, will carry out the decisions arrived at, and apply the laws enacted by, this world legislature, and will safeguard the organic unity of the whole commonwealth. A world tribunal will adjudicate and deliver its compulsory and final verdict in all and any disputes that may arise between the various elements constituting this universal system.... The economic resources of the world will be organized, its sources of raw materials will be tapped and fully utilized, its markets will be coördinated and developed, and the distribution of its products will be equitably regulated.[61]

Writing a definitive interpretation of the Administrative Order in "The Dispensation of Bahá'u'lláh", Shoghi Effendi made particular reference to the role that the institution he himself represented would play in enabling the Cause "to take a long, an uninterrupted view over a series of generations...." This unique endowment expressed itself with particular clarity in his description of the dual nature of the historical process that he saw unfolding in the twentieth century. The landscape of international affairs would, he said, be increasingly reshaped by twin forces of "integration" and "disintegration", both of them ultimately beyond human control. In the light of what meets our eyes today, his previsioning of the operation of this dual process is breathtaking: the creation of "a mechanism of world inter-communication ... functioning with marvellous swiftness and perfect regularity";[62] the undermining of the nation-state as the chief arbiter of human destiny; the devastating effects that advancing moral breakdown throughout the world would have on social cohesion; the widespread public disillusionment produced by political corruption; and—unimaginable to others of his generation—the rise of global agencies dedicated to promoting human welfare, coordinating economic activity, defining international standards, and encouraging a sense of solidarity among diverse races and cultures. These and other developments, the Guardian explained, would fundamentally alter the conditions in which the Bahá'í Cause would pursue its mission in the decades lying ahead.

One of the striking developments of this kind that Shoghi Effendi discerned in the Writings he was called on to interpret concerned the future role of the United States as a nation, and, to a lesser extent, its sister nations in the Western hemisphere. His foresight is all the more remarkable when one remembers that he was writing during a period of history when the United States was determinedly isolationist in both its foreign policy and the convictions of the majority of its citizens. Shoghi Effendi, however, envisioned the country assuming an "active and decisive part ... in the organization and the peaceful settlement of the affairs of mankind". He reminded Bahá'ís of 'Abdu'l-Bahá's anticipation that, because of the unique nature of its social composition and political development —as opposed to any "inherent excellence or special merit" of its people— the United States had developed capacities that could empower it to be "the first nation to establish the foundation of international agreement". Indeed, he foresaw the governments and peoples of the entire hemisphere becoming increasingly oriented in this direction.[63]

The role that the Bahá'í community must play in helping bring about this consummation of the historical process had been prefigured in the summons addressed to His followers by the Báb, at the very birth of the Cause:

> O My beloved friends! You are the bearers of the name of God in this Day…. You are the lowly, of whom God has thus spoken in His Book: "And We desire to show favour to those who were brought low in the land, and to make them spiritual leaders among men, and to make them Our heirs." You have been called to this station; you will attain to it, only if you arise to trample beneath your feet every earthly desire, and endeavour to become those "honoured servants of His who speak not till He hath spoken, and who do His bidding".… Heed not your weaknesses and frailty; fix your gaze upon the invincible power of the Lord, your God, the Almighty…. Arise in His name, put your trust wholly in Him, and be assured of ultimate victory.[64]

As early as 1923, Shoghi Effendi was moved to open his heart on this subject to the friends in North America:

> Let us pray to God that in these days of world-encircling gloom, when the dark forces of nature, of hate, rebellion, anarchy and reaction are threatening the very stability of human society, when the most precious fruits of civilization are undergoing severe and unparalleled tests, we may all realize, more profoundly than ever, that though but a mere handful amidst the seething masses of the world, we are in this day the chosen instruments of God's grace, that our mission is most urgent and vital to the fate of humanity, and, fortified by these sentiments, arise to achieve God's holy purpose for mankind.[65]

Fully aware of the condition into which society had fallen, the consequences of his betrayal at the hands of family members on whose assistance he should have been able to rely, and the relative weakness of

the resources available to him in the Bahá'í community itself, Shoghi
Effendi arose to forge the means needed to realize the mission bequeathed to him.

To one degree or another, most Bahá'ís no doubt appreciated that the
Assemblies they were being called on to form had a significance far beyond the mere management of practical affairs with which they were
charged. 'Abdu'l-Bahá, who had guided this development, had spoken of
them as:

> …shining lamps and heavenly gardens, from which the fragrances of
> holiness are diffused over all regions, and the lights of knowledge are
> shed abroad over all created things. From them the spirit of life
> streameth in every direction. They, indeed, are the potent sources of
> the progress of man, at all times and under all conditions.[66]

It fell to Shoghi Effendi, however, to assist the community to understand
the place and role of these national and local consultative bodies in the
framework of the Administrative Order created by Bahá'u'lláh and elaborated in the provisions of the Master's Will and Testament. An obstacle
faced by a significant number of believers in this respect was the
unexamined assumption of many that the Cause was essentially a "spiritual" association in which organization, while not necessarily antithetical,
did not constitute an inherent feature of the Divine purpose. Emphasizing
that the Kitáb-i-Aqdas and the Will and Testament "are not only complementary, but … mutually confirm one another, and are inseparable parts of
one complete unit",[67] the Guardian invited the believers to reflect deeply
on a central truth of the Cause they had embraced:

> Few will fail to recognize that the Spirit breathed by Bahá'u'lláh
> upon the world, and which is manifesting itself with varying degrees
> of intensity through the efforts consciously displayed by His avowed
> supporters and indirectly through certain humanitarian organiza-
> tions, can never permeate and exercise an abiding influence upon
> mankind unless and until it incarnates itself in a visible Order, which
> would bear His name, wholly identify itself with His principles, and
> function in conformity with His laws.[68]

He went on to urge the Faith's followers to realize the essential difference between the Cause of Bahá'u'lláh, whose Revealed Texts contain
detailed provisions for such an authoritative Order, and those preparatory Revelations whose Scriptures had been largely silent on the
administration of affairs and on the interpretation of their Founders'
intent. In the words of Bahá'u'lláh: "The Prophetic Cycle hath, verily,
ended. The Eternal Truth is now come. He hath lifted up the Ensign of
Power...."[69] Unlike the Dispensations of the past, the Revelation of
God to this age has given birth, Shoghi Effendi said, to "a living organism", whose laws and institutions constitute "the essentials of a Divine
Economy", "a pattern for future society", and "the one agency for the
unification of the world, and the proclamation of the reign of right-
eousness and justice upon the earth".[70]

The friends should strive to appreciate, therefore, the Guardian
urged, that the Spiritual Assemblies they were painstakingly establishing
throughout the world were the forerunners of the local and national
"Houses of Justice" envisioned by Bahá'u'lláh. As such, they were integral
parts of an Administrative Order that will, in time, "assert its claim and
demonstrate its capacity to be regarded not only as the nucleus but the
very pattern of the New World Order destined to embrace in the fullness
of time the whole of mankind".[71]

For a few in the young communities of the West, such a departure
from traditional conceptions of the nature and role of religion proved too
great a test, and Bahá'í communities suffered the distress of seeing valued
co-workers drift away in search of spiritual pursuits more congenial to
their inclinations. For the vast majority of believers, however, great messages from the Guardian's pen, such as "The Goal of a New World Order"
and "The Dispensation of Bahá'u'lláh", threw brilliant light on precisely
the issue that most concerned them, the relationship between spiritual
truth and social development, inspiring in them a determination to play
their part in laying the foundations of humanity's future.

The Guardian provided, as well, the organizing image for this mighty
work. The "Heroic Age" of Bahá'u'lláh's Dispensation, he declared, had
ended with the passing of 'Abdu'l-Bahá. The Bahá'í community now embarked on the "Iron Age", the "Formative Age", in which the

Administrative Order would be erected throughout the planet, its institutions established and the "society building" powers inherent in it fully revealed. Far ahead lay what Shoghi Effendi called the "Golden Age" of the Dispensation, leading eventually to the emergence of the Bahá'í World Commonwealth that will constitute the establishment on earth of the Kingdom of God and the creation of a world civilization.[72] The impulse that had been initially communicated to human consciousness through the revelation of the Creative Word itself, whose revolutionary social implications had been proclaimed by the Master, was now being translated by their appointed interpreter into the vocabulary of political and economic transformation in which the public discourse of the century was everywhere taking place. Lending the process irresistible force, illuminating ever new dimensions of Bahá'í experience, and serving as the mainspring of the unification of humankind it proclaimed was the Covenant that Bahá'u'lláh had established between Himself and those who turn to Him.

Although not initially designated "Spiritual Assemblies", the councils that local Bahá'í communities in Persia had been encouraged by 'Abdu'l-Bahá to create had assumed responsibility for the administration of their affairs. In the light of what was to follow, no one with a sense of history can fail to be struck by the fact that the Faith's first Spiritual Assembly, that of Tehran, was founded in 1897, the year of Shoghi Effendi's own birth. Under the Master's guidance, intermittent meetings held by the four Hands of the Cause in Persia had gradually evolved into this institution that served simultaneously as Persia's "Central Spiritual Assembly" and as the governing body of the local community in the capital. By the time of 'Abdu'l-Bahá's passing, there were more than thirty Local Spiritual Assemblies established in Persia. In 1922 Shoghi Effendi called for the formal establishment of Persia's National Spiritual Assembly, an achievement delayed until 1934 by the demands related to the taking of a reliable census of the community as a basis for the election of delegates.

Outside Persia, the believers in 'Ishqábád, in Russian Turkestan, elected their first Local Spiritual Assembly, a body that assumed an important role in the project for the construction of the first Bahá'í Mashriqu'l-Adhkár in 'Ishqábád. In North America a variety of consultative arrangements—"Boards of Council", "Council Boards", "Boards of

Consultation" and "Working Committees"—performed analogous functions, evolving gradually into elected bodies that constituted the forerunners of Spiritual Assemblies. By the time of the Master's passing, there were perhaps forty such councils functioning in North America. These developments prepared the way for the eventual emergence of the first National Spiritual Assembly of the Bahá'ís of the United States and Canada, which evolved from the "Temple Unity Board", a body created in 1909 to coordinate construction of the future House of Worship. It was formed in 1923, although the administrative requirements set by the Guardian for this step were met only in 1925. Before this latter date arrived, National Assemblies had been established in the British Isles, in Germany and Austria, in India and Burma, and in Egypt and the Sudan.[73]

As the formation of National and Local Spiritual Assemblies was taking place, the Guardian began to lay emphasis on the importance of their securing recognition as "corporate persons" under civil law. By securing such formal incorporation, in whatever fashion proved practicable, Bahá'í administrative institutions would be enabled to hold property, enter into contracts, and gradually assume a range of legal rights vital to the interests of the Cause. The importance Shoghi Effendi attached to this new stage of administrative evolution becomes clear in the photocopies of such civil instruments that began to become a major feature of the photographic coverage of the expansion of the Faith in successive volumes of *The Bahá'í World*. Indeed, once the Mansion at Bahjí had been repossessed and fully restored to its original condition, and appropriately furnished, Shoghi Effendi put together a collection of this much valued documentation for display there as an encouragement and education for the growing stream of pilgrims to the World Centre.

The processes of civil incorporation began with the adoption in 1927 of a Declaration of Trust and By-Laws for the National Spiritual Assembly of the United States and Canada, which gained civil recognition as a voluntary trust two years later. On 17 February 1932 the first local Bahá'í Assembly, that of Chicago, adopted papers of incorporation which, together with those adopted by that of New York City on 31 March of that year, were to become a pattern for such instruments throughout the world. By 1949, the National Spiritual Assembly of the Bahá'ís of

Canada—formed when the two North American Bahá'í communities had separated the previous year—was able to secure formal recognition of its status under civil law through a special Act of Parliament, a victory which Shoghi Effendi hailed as "an act wholly unprecedented in the annals of the Faith in any country, in either East or West".[74]

These pressing administrative demands did not distract Shoghi Effendi from other tasks that were vital to shaping the spiritual life of a global community. The most important of these was the arduous work that he alone could perform in providing the growing body of the believers who were not of Persian background with direct and reliable access to the Writings of the Faith's Founders. The Hidden Words, The Kitáb-i-Íqán, the priceless treasury brought together with so much love and insight under the title *Gleanings from the Writings of Bahá'u'lláh*, *Prayers and Meditations of Bahá'u'lláh* and Epistle to the Son of the Wolf provided the spiritual nourishment the work of the Cause urgently required, as did Shoghi Effendi's translation and editing of Nabíl's "Narrative" under the title *The Dawn-Breakers*.

Bahá'í pilgrims found spiritual enrichment of yet another kind in the Holy Places and historic sites that the Guardian acquired—often at the cost of protracted and wrenching negotiations—and lovingly restored. Shoghi Effendi was equally responsive to unexpected opportunities that offered themselves to his historical perspective. In 1925, a Sunni Muslim religious court in Egypt denied civil recognition to marriages contracted between Muslim women and Bahá'í men, insisting that "The Bahá'í Faith is a new religion, entirely independent" and that "no Bahá'í, therefore, can be regarded a Muslim" (and therefore qualified to enter into marriage with someone who was).[75] Seizing on the larger implications of this apparent defeat, the Guardian made wide use of the court's definitive judgement to reinforce the claim of the Cause in international circles to be an independent Faith, separate and distinct from its Islamic roots.

As the Bahá'í community was constructing administrative foundations which would permit it to play an effective role in human affairs, the

accelerating process of disintegration that Shoghi Effendi had discerned
was undermining the fabric of social order. Its origins, however determinedly ignored by many social and political theorists, are beginning,
after the lapse of several decades, to gain recognition at international conferences devoted to peace and development. In our own time, it is no
longer unusual to encounter in such circles candid references to the essential role that "spiritual" and "moral" forces must play in achieving
solutions to urgent problems. For a Bahá'í reader, such belated recognition awakens echoes of warning addressed over a century earlier by
Bahá'u'lláh to the rulers of human affairs: "The vitality of men's belief in
God is dying out in every land.... The corrosion of ungodliness is eating
into the vitals of human society...."[76]

The responsibility for this greatest of tragedies, the Guardian emphasized, rests primarily on the shoulders of the world's religious
leaders. Bahá'u'lláh's severest condemnation is reserved for those who,
presuming to speak in God's name, have imposed on credulous masses
a welter of dogmas and prejudices that have constituted the greatest single obstacle against which the advancement of civilization has been
forced to struggle. While acknowledging the humanitarian services of
countless individual clerics, He points out the consequences of the way
in which self-appointed religious elites, throughout history, have inter-
posed themselves between humanity and all voices of progress, not
excluding the Messengers of God Themselves. "What 'oppression' is
more grievous," He asks, "than that a soul seeking the truth, and wish-
ing to attain unto the knowledge of God, should know not where to go
for it...?"[77] In an age of scientific advancement and widespread popular education, the cumulative effects of the resulting disillusionment
were to make religious faith appear irrelevant. Impotent themselves to
deal with the spiritual crisis, most of those clerics of various Faiths who
became aware of Bahá'u'lláh's message either ignored the moral influence it was demonstrating or actively opposed it.[78]

Recognition of this feature of history does not diminish the harm
done by those who have sought to take advantage of the spiritual vacuum
thus left. The yearning for belief is inextinguishable, an inherent part of
what makes one human. When it is blocked or betrayed, the rational soul

is driven to seek some new compass point, however inadequate or unworthy, around which it can organize experience and dare again to assume the risks that are an inescapable aspect of life. It was in this perspective that Shoghi Effendi warned the members of the Faith, in unusually strong language, that they must try to understand the spiritual calamity engulfing a large part of humankind during the decades between the two world wars:

> God Himself has indeed been dethroned from the hearts of men, and an idolatrous world passionately and clamorously hails and worships the false gods which its own idle fancies have fatuously created, and its misguided hands so impiously exalted…. Their high priests are the politicians and the worldly-wise, the so-called sages of the age; their sacrifice, the flesh and blood of the slaughtered multitudes; their incantations, outworn shibboleths and insidious and irreverent formulas; their incense, the smoke of anguish that ascends from the lacerated hearts of the bereaved, the maimed, and the homeless.[79]

Like opportunistic infections, aggressive ideologies took advantage of the situation created by the decline of religious vitality. Although indistinguishable from one another in the corruption of faith they represented, the three belief systems that played a dominant role in human affairs during the twentieth century differed sharply in their secondary and more conspicuous characteristics to which the Guardian drew attention. In denouncing "the dark, the false, and crooked doctrines" that would bring devastation on "any man or people who believes in them", Shoghi Effendi warned particularly against "the triple gods of Nationalism, Racialism and Communism".[80]

Of Fascism's founding regime, created by the so-called "March on Rome" in 1922, little need be said. Long before it and its leader had been swept into oblivion during the concluding months of the second world war, Fascism had become an object of ridicule among the majority of even those who had originally supported it. Its significance lies, rather, in the host of imitators it spawned and which were to proliferate throughout the world like some malignant series of mutations, in the decades since then. Fuelled by a manic nationalism, this aberration of the human spirit deified the state, discovered everywhere imaginary threats to the national survival of whatever unhappy people it had fastened upon, and preached to all who would listen the notion that war has an "ennobling" influence on the human soul. The comic opera parade of uniforms, jackboots, banners and trumpets usually associated with it should not conceal from a contemporary observer the virulent legacy it has left in our own age, enshrining in political vocabulary such anguished terms as *desaparecidos* ("the disappeared").

While sharing Fascism's idolatry of the state, its sister ideology Naziism made itself the voice of a far more ancient and insidious perversion. At its dark heart was an obsession with what its proponents called "race purity". The single-minded determination with which it pursued its murderous ends was in no way weakened by the demonstrably false postulates upon which it was based. The Nazi system was unique in the sheer bestiality of the act most commonly associated with its name, the programme of genocide systematically carried out against populations considered either valueless or harmful to humanity's future, a programme that included a deliberate attempt literally to exterminate the entire Jewish people. Ultimately, it was Naziism's determination that a "master race" of its own conception must rule over the entire planet which was principally responsible for fulfilling 'Abdu'l-Bahá's prophetic warning of twenty years earlier that another war, far more terrible than the first, would ravage the world. Like Fascism, Naziism has left a detritus in our own time. In its case, this takes the form of a language and symbols through which fringe elements in present-day society, demoralized by the economic and social decay around them and made desperate by the absence of solutions, vent their impotent rage on minorities whom they blame for their disappointments.

The false god that the Master was moved to identify explicitly, and the one denounced by name by Shoghi Effendi, had demonstrated its character at its outset by brutally destroying, during the latter part of World War I, the first democratic government ever established in Russia. For long years, the Soviet system created by Vladimir Lenin succeeded in representing itself to many as a benefactor of humankind and the champion of social justice. In the light of historical events, such pretensions were grotesque. The documentation now available provides irrefutable evidence of crimes so enormous and follies so abysmal as to have no parallel in the six thousand years of recorded history. To a degree never before imagined, let alone attempted, the Leninist conspiracy against human nature also sought systematically to extinguish faith in God. Whatever view of the situation political theorists may currently hold, no one can be surprised that such deliberate violence to the roots of human motivation led inexorably to the economic and political ruin of those societies luckless enough to fall under Soviet sway. Its longer-term spiritual effect, tragically, was to pervert to the service of its own amoral agenda the legitimate yearnings for freedom and justice of subject peoples throughout the world.

From a Bahá'í point of view, humanity's worship of idols of its own invention is of importance not because of the historical events associated with these forces, however horrifying, but because of the lesson it taught. Looking back on the twilight world in which such diabolical forces loomed over humanity's future, one must ask what was the weakness in human nature that rendered it vulnerable to such influences. To have seen in someone like Benito Mussolini the figure of a "Man of Destiny", to have felt obliged to understand the racial theories of Adolf Hitler as anything other than the self-evident products of a diseased mind, to have seriously entertained the reinterpretation of human experience through dogmas that had given birth to the Soviet Union of Josef Stalin—so wilful an abandonment of reason on the part of a considerable segment of the intellectual leadership of society demands an accounting to posterity. If undertaken dispassionately, such an evaluation must, sooner or later, focus attention on a truth that runs like a central strand through the Scriptures of all of humanity's religions. In the words of Bahá'u'lláh:

> Upon the reality of man ... He hath focused the radiance of all of His names and attributes, and made it a mirror of His own Self.... These energies ... lie, however, latent within him, even as the flame is hidden within the candle and the rays of light are potentially present in the lamp.... Neither the candle nor the lamp can be lighted through

their own unaided efforts, nor can it ever be possible for the mirror to free itself from its dross.[81]

The consequence of humanity's infatuation with the ideologies its own mind had conceived was to produce a terrifying acceleration of the process of disintegration that was dissolving the fabric of social life and cultivating the basest impulses of human nature. The brutalization that the first world war had engendered now became an omnipresent feature of social life throughout much of the planet. "Thus have We gathered together the workers of iniquity", Bahá'u'lláh warned over a century earlier. "We see them rushing on towards their idol.... They hasten forward to Hell Fire, and mistake it for light."[82]

VI

WITH THE ADMINISTRATIVE STRUCTURE of the Cause taking shape, Shoghi Effendi turned his attention to the task he had been compelled to delay for so long, the implementation of the Master's Divine Plan. In Persia, the development was already well advanced. Directed first by Bahá'u'lláh and subsequently by 'Abdu'l-Bahá, a corps of especially designated teachers—*muballighín*—stimulated the work at the local level throughout the country, and the existence of a vibrant community life assisted in the relatively rapid integration of new declarants. Ḥuqúqu'lláh funds, supplemented by the practice of deputization, which was already an established feature of Persian Bahá'í consciousness, provided material support for this teaching activity.

In the West, inspiration for the promotion of the Faith had been provided by the response to the Master's appeals by such outstanding individuals as Lua Getsinger, May Maxwell and Martha Root. Merely to mention these names is to highlight a feature of the rise of the Cause in the West to which the Master drew particular attention:

> In America, the women have outdone the men in this regard and have taken the lead in this field. They strive harder in guiding the

peoples of the world, and their endeavours are greater. They are confirmed by divine bestowals and blessings.[83]

In the East, social conditions of the time had virtually dictated that the initiative in the promotion of the Cause would be taken largely by men. Few such constraints prevailed in North America and Europe, where a galaxy of unforgettable women became the principal exponents of the Bahá'í message on both sides of the Atlantic. One thinks of Sarah Farmer, whose Green Acre school provided the infant Bahá'í community with a forum for the introduction of the Faith to influential thinkers; of Sara Lady Blomfield, whose social position lent added force to the ardour with which she championed the teachings; of Marion Jack, immortalized by Shoghi Effendi as a model for Bahá'í pioneers; of Laura Dreyfus-Barney, who gave the Faith the priceless collection of the Master's table talks, *Some Answered Questions*; of Agnes Parsons, co-founder with Louis Gregory of the "Race Amity" initiatives inspired by 'Abdu'l-Bahá; of Corinne True, Keith Ransom-Kehler, Helen Goodall, Juliet Thompson, Grace Ober, Ethel Rosenberg, Clara Dunn, Alma Knobloch and a distinguished company of others, most of whom pioneered some new field of Bahá'í service.

To the list must be added the name of Queen Marie of Romania, whom the ages will hail as the first crowned head to recognize the Revelation of God for this day. The courage shown by this lone woman in publicly declaring her faith, through the letters she fearlessly addressed to the editors of several newspapers in both Europe and North America, in all probability introduced the name of the Cause to an audience numbering millions of readers.

Despite the impressive response that the earliest of these efforts elicited, the lack of an organized means of capitalizing on the results initially limited the benefits accruing to Bahá'í communities in Western lands. The rise of the Administrative Order dramatically changed the latter situation. As Local Spiritual Assemblies came into being, goals were set, resources were made available to support individual teaching efforts, and those who declared their faith found themselves participating in the many activities of an engrossing Bahá'í community life. It was now possible to systematically translate and publish literature, news of general interest was regularly shared, and the bonds that linked believers with the World Centre of the Faith grew steadily stronger.

The two chief instruments by which Shoghi Effendi set about cultivating a heightened devotion to teaching in both East and West were the same as those on which the Master had relied. A steady stream of letters to communities and individuals alike opened up for the recipients new dimensions in the beliefs they had embraced. The most important of these communications, however, now became those addressed to National and Local Spiritual Assemblies. Their effect was intensified by the stream of returning pilgrims who shared insights gained by direct contact with the Centre of the Cause. Through these connections every individual believer was encouraged to see himself or herself as an instrument of the power flowing through the Covenant. The invaluable compilation that eventually appeared under the title *Messages to America, 1932-1946* provides a review of the steps by which Shoghi Effendi drew the North American believers ever deeper into the implications of the Master's Divine Plan for "the spiritual conquest of the planet":

> By the sublimity and serenity of their faith, by the steadiness and clarity of their vision, the incorruptibility of their character, the rigor of their discipline, the sanctity of their morals, and the unique example of their community life, they can and indeed must in a world polluted with its incurable corruptions, paralyzed by its haunting fears, torn by its devastating hatreds, and languishing under the weight of its appalling miseries demonstrate the validity of their claim to be regarded as the sole repository of that grace upon whose operation must depend the complete deliverance, the fundamental reorganization and the supreme felicity of all mankind.[84]

The Guardian held up before the eyes of the North American Bahá'í community a vision of their spiritual destiny. Its members were, he said, "the spiritual descendants of the heroes of God's Cause", their rising institutions were "the visible symbols of its [the Faith's] undoubted sovereignty", the teachers and pioneers it sent out were "torch-bearers of an as yet unborn civilization", it was their collective challenge to assume "a preponderating share" in laying the foundations of the World Order "which the

Báb has heralded, which the mind of Bahá'u'lláh has envisioned, and whose
features 'Abdu'l-Bahá, its Architect, has delineated...."[85]

The language of the messages is magnificent, enthralling. In acknowledging the darkness that widespread godlessness, violence and
creeping immorality was engendering, Shoghi Effendi described the role
that Bahá'ís everywhere must play as instruments of the transforming
power of the new Revelation:

> Theirs is the duty to hold, aloft and undimmed, the torch of Divine
> guidance, as the shades of night descend upon, and ultimately en-
> velop the entire human race. Theirs is the function, amidst its
> tumults, perils and agonies, to witness to the vision, and proclaim the
> approach, of that re-created society, that Christ-promised Kingdom,
> that World Order whose generative impulse is the spirit of none other
> than Bahá'u'lláh Himself, whose dominion is the entire planet, whose
> watchword is unity, whose animating power is the force of Justice,
> whose directive purpose is the reign of righteousness and truth, and
> whose supreme glory is the complete, the undisturbed and everlasting
> felicity of the whole of human kind.[86]

In 1936 the Guardian judged that the administrative structure of the
Cause was sufficiently broad and consolidated in North America that he
could begin the first stage of the implementation of the Divine Plan itself.
With the world sliding into another global conflagration, and the scope
possible to the efforts of the Persian believers being severely limited, the
focus would necessarily have to be on the expansion and consolidation of
the Bahá'í community in the Western hemisphere in preparation for the
much larger undertakings that lay ahead. Calling on the Plan's appointed
"executors", the believers in North America, the Guardian laid out a Seven
Year Plan, scheduled to run from 1937 to 1944. Its objectives were to establish at least one Local Spiritual Assembly in every state of the United
States and every province of Canada, and to open to the Cause fourteen
republics in Latin America. To these objectives was added the task, im-
mensely demanding of a community with still very limited numbers and
severely straitened financial resources, of completing the exterior ornamen-
tation of the "Mother Temple of the West".

Rúḥíyyih Khánum has pointed out a striking parallel between two developments during this period of history. On the one hand, powerful nations were launching armies of invasion whose goal was to seize the natural resources of neighbour states—or simply to satisfy an appetite for conquest. During this same period, Shoghi Effendi was mobilizing the painfully small band of pioneers available to him, and dispatching them to the teaching goals of the Plan he had created. Within a few short years, the vast battalions of aggression would be shattered beyond recovery, their names and conquests erased from history. The little company of believers who had gone out with their lives in their hands to fulfil the mission entrusted to them by the Guardian would have achieved or exceeded all of their objectives, objectives that soon became the foundations of flourishing communities.[87]

In appreciating this undertaking, it is helpful for Bahá'ís to understand not only the role that planning plays in the life of the Cause, but the unique nature of this instrumentality in its Bahá'í expression. The systematic identification of objectives to be achieved and decisions as to how to achieve them does not mean that the Bahá'í community has assumed the responsibility of "designing" a future for itself, as the concept of planning customarily implies. What Bahá'í institutions do, rather, is to strive to align the work of the Cause with the Divinely impelled process they see steadily unfolding in the world, a process that will ultimately realize its purpose, regardless of historical circumstances or events. The challenge to the Administrative Order is to ensure that, as Providence allows, Bahá'í efforts are in harmony with this Greater Plan of God, because it is in doing so that the potentialities implanted in the Cause by Bahá'u'lláh bear their fruit. That the provisions of the Kitáb-i-Aqdas and the Will and Testament of 'Abdu'l-Bahá ensure the success of the efforts of the Bahá'ís is dramatically demonstrated in the unbroken series of triumphs that fulfilled the plans created by Shoghi Effendi.

By August 1944, Shoghi Effendi was able to celebrate the completion of the first Seven Year Plan. The Guardian marked the moment with a gift to the Bahá'ís of the world that represents one of the greatest achievements of his life. The publication, in 1944, of *God Passes By*, his comprehensive and reflective history of the first hundred years of the

Cause, threw open for believers a window on the spiritual process by which Bahá'u'lláh's purpose for humankind is being realized.

History is a powerful instrument. At its best, it provides a perspective on the past and casts a light on the future. It populates human consciousness with heroes, saints and martyrs whose example awakens in everyone touched by it capacities they had not imagined they possessed. It helps make sense of the world—and of human experience. It inspires, consoles and enlightens. It enriches life. In the great body of literature and legend that it has left to humanity, history's hand can be seen at work shaping much of the course of civilization—in the legends that have inspired the ideals of every people since the dawn of recorded time, as well as in the epics of the *Ramayana*, in the exploits celebrated in the *Odyssey* and the *Aeneid*, in the Nordic sagas, in the *Shahnameh*, and in much of the Bible and the Qur'án.

God Passes By elevates this great work of the mind to a level ardently striven after but never attained in any of ages past. Those who open themselves to its vision discover in it an avenue of approach to understanding the Purpose of God, an avenue that converges with the vast expanse spread out in the Guardian's matchless translations of the Revealed Texts. Its appearance on the centenary of the birth of the Cause —just as the Bahá'í world was celebrating the success of the first collective effort it had ever been able to undertake—summoned up for believers everywhere the full majesty and meaning of a hundred years of ceaseless sacrifice.

At a relatively early point in the second world war, the Guardian set that conflict in a perspective for Bahá'ís that was very different from the one generally prevailing. The war should be regarded, he said, "as the direct continuation" of the conflagration ignited in 1914. It would come to be seen as the "essential pre-requisite to world unification". The entry into the war by the United States, whose president had initiated the project of a system of international order, but which had itself rejected this visionary initiative, would lead that nation, Shoghi Effendi predicted, to "assume through adversity its preponderating share of responsibility to lay down, once for all, broad, worldwide, unassailable foundations of that discredited yet immortal System."[88]

These statements proved prophetic. With the end of hostilities, it gradually became apparent that a fundamental shift in consciousness was under way throughout the world and that inherited assumptions, institutions and priorities that had been progressively undermined by forces at work during the first half of the century were now crumbling. If the change could not yet be described as an emerging conviction about the oneness of humankind, no objective observer could mistake the fact that barriers blocking such a realization, which had survived all the assaults against them earlier in the century, were at last giving way. One's mind turns to the prophetic words of the Qur'án: "And you see the mountains and think them solid, but they shall pass away as the passing away of the clouds." (27:88) The effect was to inspire in progressive minds a sense of confidence that it would be possible to construct a new kind of society that would not only preserve the long-term peace of the world, but enrich the lives of all of its inhabitants.

Primarily, this new birth of hope had resulted, as Shoghi Effendi had foreseen, from the "fiery ordeal" that had at last succeeded in "implanting that sense of responsibility" which leaders earlier in the century had sought to avoid.[89] To this new awareness had been added the effects of the fear induced by the invention and use of atomic weapons, a reaction calling to mind for Bahá'ís the Master's prescient statements in North America that ultimately peace would come because the nations would be driven to accept it. The *Montreal Daily Star* had quoted Him as saying: "It [peace] will be universal in the twentieth century. All nations will be forced into it."[90] The years immediately following 1945 witnessed advances in framing a new social order that went far beyond the brightest hopes of earlier decades.

Most important of all was the willingness of national governments to create a new system of international order, and to endow it with the peacekeeping authority so tragically denied to the defunct League. Meeting in San Francisco in April 1945—in the state where 'Abdu'l-Bahá had prophetically declared, "May the first flag of international peace be upraised in this state"—delegates of fifty nations adopted the Charter of the United Nations Organization, the name proposed for it by President Franklin D. Roosevelt.[91] Ratification by the required number of member nations followed that October, and the first General Assembly of the new organization convened on 10 January 1946, in London. In October 1949, the cornerstone of the United Nations' permanent seat was laid in New York City, hailed by 'Abdu'l-Bahá thirty-seven years earlier as the "City of the Covenant". During His visit there He had predicted: "There is no doubt that … the banner of international agreement will be unfurled here to spread onward and outward among all the nations of the world."[92]

Significantly, it was also on the initiative of a political leader of one of the Western hemisphere nations which had been addressed by Bahá'u'lláh, that His summons to collective security—first reflected in the nominal sanctions voted by the League of Nations against Fascist aggression in Ethiopia—was at long last given practical effect. In November 1956, Lester Bowles Pearson, then External Affairs Minister and later Prime Minister of Canada, secured the creation by the United Nations of its first international peacekeeping force, an achievement which won its author the Nobel Prize for Peace.[93] The full nature of the authority contained in such a mandate would steadily emerge as a major feature of international relations during the second half of the century. Beginning with the policing of agreements worked out between hostile states, the principle of collective action in defence of peace gradually took on the form of military interventions such as that of the Gulf War, in which compliance with Security Council resolutions was imposed by force on aggressor factions and states.

Along with the establishment of the new United Nations' system and steps to enforce its sanctions, a second major breakthrough occurred. Even before hostilities had ended, public audiences throughout the world were stunned by film coverage of the liberation of Nazi death camps, which exposed for all to see the horrific consequences of racism. What can adequately be described only as a profound sense of shame at the depths of evil that humanity had shown itself capable of committing shook the conscience of humankind. Through the window of opportunity thus briefly opened, a group of dedicated and far-sighted men and women, under the inspired leadership of figures like Eleanor Roosevelt, secured the United Nations' adoption of the Universal Declaration of Human Rights. The moral commitment it represented was institutionalized in the subsequent establishment of the United Nations Commission on Human Rights. In due course, the Bahá'í community itself would have good cause to appreciate, at firsthand, the system's importance as a shield protecting minorities from the abuses of the past.

Highlighting the significance of both advances was the decision of the nations that had triumphed in the recent conflict to put on trial leading figures of the Nazi regime. For the first time in history, the leaders of a sovereign nation—men who sought to argue the constitutionality of the political positions they had occupied—were brought before a public court, their crimes unsparingly reviewed and documented, were duly convicted, and those who did not escape through suicide were then either hanged or sentenced to long terms of imprisonment. No serious protest had been raised against this procedure which, theoretically, constituted a fundamental departure from existing norms of international law. Although the integrity of the proceedings was gravely marred by the participation of judges appointed by a Soviet dictatorship whose own crimes matched or exceeded those of the defendants' regime, the act set an historic precedent. It demonstrated, for the first time, that the fetish of "national sovereignty" has recognizable and enforceable limits.

Beginning in these same years, the fulfilment of a long-delayed ideal unfolded in the dissolution of the great empires that had not merely survived 1918, but had managed even to extend their reach through acquiring "mandates", "protectorates" and colonies seized from the defeated powers. Now, these antiquated systems of political oppression were submerged by a rising tide of movements of national liberation far beyond their weakened abilities to resist. With astonishing swiftness, all of them either willingly abandoned their claims or were forced by colonial rebellions to bow to the same fate that had overtaken their Ottoman and Hapsburg predecessors earlier in the century.

Suddenly, the peoples of the world found themselves with a place to stand in dignity, a forum in which to express the concerns that most deeply affected them, and the faint beginnings of a role in deciding their own future and that of humanity in general. A corner had been turned that left behind six or more millennia of history. Beyond all the continuing educational disadvantages, the economic inequities, and the obstructions created by political and diplomatic manœuvring—beyond all these practical but historically transient limitations—a new authority was at work in human affairs to which all might reasonably hope somehow to appeal. Representatives of once subject peoples, whose exotically clad warriors had brought up the rear of the Diamond Jubilee procession in London only five decades earlier, now began to appear as delegates to the Security Council and occupants of senior posts in the United Nations and non-governmental organizations of every kind. The magnitude of the change is perhaps best symbolized by the fact that the Secretary-General of the United Nations is today a Ghanaian, his two immediate predecessors having been, respectively, from Egypt and Peru.[94]

Nor was this change merely one of formal and administrative character. As time passed, growing numbers of outstanding figures in every walk of life would escape the familiar limits of racial, cultural or religious identity. In every continent of the globe, names like Anne Frank, Martin Luther King Jr., Paolo Freire, Ravi Shankar, Gabriel García Marques, Kiri Te Kanawa, Andrei Sakharov, Mother Teresa and Zhang Yimou became sources of inspiration and encouragement to great numbers of their fellow citizens.[95] In every department of life, heroism, professional excellence or moral distinction would increasingly be able to speak for themselves and be embraced by the generality of humankind. The world-wide outpouring of affection and rejoicing that was to greet the release from prison of Nelson Mandela and his subsequent election as president of his country would reflect a sense among peoples of every race and nation that these historic events represented victories of the human family itself.

It became apparent, too, that pre-war conceptions regarding the use and distribution of wealth would have to be overhauled. Apart from principles of social justice, which doubtless motivated a significant number of those committed to this task, the economic dislocations

produced by the events of the previous three decades had made it clear
that existing arrangements were outdated and ineffective. Experiments
to address such problems at the national level had been undertaken in
several countries in response to the Depression during the 1930s. Now
an interlocking system of institutions oriented to recognition that national economies constitute elements of a global whole was successively
devised and put in place. The International Monetary Fund, the General Agreement on Tariffs and Trades, the World Bank, and various
subsidiary agencies began belatedly to grapple with the implications of
an integrating world, and with issues related to the distribution of
wealth inherent in this development. Thinkers in developing countries
were not slow to point out that such initiatives served primarily the
needs of the Western world. Nevertheless, their emergence marked a
fundamental change of direction that would increasingly open participation to a wide range of states and institutions.

A humanitarian initiative of a kind never previously conceived
opened still another dimension of the global integration occurring. Beginning with the "Marshall Plan" devised by the government of the
United States to rehabilitate war-torn European nations, those nations
that were able to do so turned to serious consideration of programmes
that might foster the social and economic development of rising nations.
Widespread publicity awakened a sense of solidarity with the rest of the
world on the part of peoples in lands that enjoyed reasonable levels of
education, health care and the application of technology. In time, this
ambitious initiative came under attack for the mixed motives attributed
to it. Nor can anyone deny that the long-term results of development
projects have been heartbreakingly disappointing in their failure to close
the yawning gap between the rich and the poor. Neither circumstance
can obscure, however, a sense of common humanity in its objectives that
spoke perhaps most eloquently in the response it evoked from an army of
idealistic youth of many lands.

Paradoxically, in the Far East particularly, even war had a certain liberating effect on consciousness. As early as 1904, the Russo-Japanese
conflict had been seen in parts of the Orient as encouraging evidence that
non-Western peoples could resist the apparently invincible might of the

West. The effect had been heightened by the events of the first world war, and greatly advanced by the success of Japanese arms in withstanding for so long the massive Western effort devoted to defeating them during the period 1941-1945. The second half of the century saw this new technological expertise give birth to modern economies in half a dozen nations of the region, whose innovative products and industrial energy, particularly in the areas of transportation and information technology, were able to hold their own with the best that the rest of the world had to offer.

By 1946, the end of hostilities had opened the way for the launching by Shoghi Effendi of a second Seven Year Plan, which benefited from the new receptivity to the message of the Faith produced by the shift of consciousness that was by then already apparent. Once again, the North American Bahá'í community was summoned to assume a demanding responsibility, one that essentially built upon and developed the achievements of the earlier Plan. The great difference, however, was that several other Bahá'í communities were now in a position to participate. Already in 1938, the Bahá'ís of India, Pakistan and Burma had set out on a plan of their own. As international hostilities gradually came to an end, the National Spiritual Assemblies of Persia, of the British Isles, of Australia and New Zealand, of Germany and Austria, of Egypt and the Sudan, and of Iraq—freed from the limitations imposed on them by the war—embarked on projects of various durations to expand the base of the Administrative Order, settle pioneers in goals both at home and abroad, and multiply the available Bahá'í literature.

By 1953 all of these undertakings had been fully completed. Three new National Spiritual Assemblies had been established and had also undertaken supplementary teaching plans, an array of new Local Spiritual Assemblies had been formed in Europe, initiatives by five different national communities acting under the coordination of the National Spiritual Assembly of the British Isles had led to the settling of pioneers in East and

West Africa, and the great project set in motion by the Master's laying of the corner stone of the Mother Temple of the West was at last finished. [96]

Before the believers could celebrate these achievements, a new challenge of staggering proportions was unveiled by Shoghi Effendi. Impelled by historic forces that only he was in a position to appreciate, the Guardian announced the launching at the forthcoming Riḍván of a decade-long, world-embracing Plan, which he designated a "Spiritual Crusade". Engaging the energies of all the twelve National Spiritual Assemblies then in existence—the twelfth being that of the Italo-Swiss community—it called for the establishment of the Faith in one hundred and thirty-one additional countries and territories, together with the formation of forty-four new National Spiritual Assemblies, the incorporation of thirty-three of these, a vast increase in Bahá'í literature, the erection of Houses of Worship in Iran and Germany (the former being replaced by Temples in both Africa and Australia when the Tehran project was blocked), and the expansion of the number of Local Spiritual Assemblies around the world to a total of five thousand, of which three hundred and fifty must be incorporated. Nothing in their collective experience had prepared the Bahá'ís of the world for so colossal an undertaking. The magnitude of the challenge was set out by Shoghi Effendi in a cablegram of 8 October 1952:

> Feel hour propitious to proclaim to the entire Bahá'í world the projected launching ... the fate-laden, soul-stirring, decade-long, world-embracing Spiritual Crusade involving ... the concerted participation of all National Spiritual Assemblies of the Bahá'í world aiming at the immediate extension of Bahá'u'lláh's spiritual dominion ... in all remaining Sovereign States, Principal Dependencies comprising Principalities, Sultanates, Emirates, Shaykhdoms, Protectorates, Trust Territories, and Crown Colonies scattered over the surface of the entire planet. The entire body of the avowed supporters of Bahá'u'lláh's all-conquering Faith are now summoned to achieve in a single decade feats eclipsing in totality the achievements which in the course of the eleven preceding decades illuminated the annals of Bahá'í pioneering. [97]

Victory in so ambitious an enterprise would mean that the embrace of the Faith would span the globe, that the institutional foundations of its Administrative Order would expand at least five-fold, and that its community life would be enriched through the participation of believers from a vast number of as yet untapped cultures, nations and tribes.

In effect, the Plan called for the Cause to make a giant leap forward over what might otherwise have been several stages in its evolution. What Shoghi Effendi saw clearly—and what only the powers of foresight inherent in the Guardianship made it possible to see—was that an historical conjunction of circumstances presented the Bahá'í community with an opportunity that would not come again and on which the success of future stages in the prosecution of the Divine Plan would entirely depend. What he did not hesitate to call the "summons of the Lord of Hosts" was embodied in a message that seized the imagination of Bahá'ís in every part of the world:

> No matter how long the period that separates them from ultimate victory; however arduous the task; however formidable the exertions demanded of them; however dark the days which mankind, perplexed and sorely-tried, must, in its hour of travail, traverse; however severe the tests with which they who are to redeem its fortunes will be confronted.... I adjure them, by the precious blood that flowed in such great profusion, by the lives of the unnumbered saints and heroes who were immolated, by the supreme, the glorious sacrifice of the Prophet-Herald of our Faith, by the tribulations which its Founder, Himself, willingly underwent, so that His Cause might live, His Order might redeem a shattered world and its glory might suffuse the entire planet—I adjure them, as this solemn hour draws nigh, to resolve never to flinch, never to hesitate, never to relax, until each and every objective in the Plans to be proclaimed, at a later date, has been fully consummated.[98]

The response was immediate. Within a few months messages from the World Centre began sharing the news of a succession of victories in country after country. Those pioneers who succeeded in establishing the Faith's first foothold in a country or territory were designated "Knights of

Bahá'u'lláh", and their names inscribed on a Roll of Honour destined, in time, to be deposited, as called for by the Guardian, under the threshold of the entrance to the Shrine of Bahá'u'lláh. Nothing testified quite so dramatically to the foresight embodied in Shoghi Effendi's successive Plans than the fact that, within each of the new nation-states born after the second world war, Bahá'í communities and Spiritual Assemblies were already a part of the fabric of national life.

A brilliant succession of achievements followed these initial ones. By October 1957, by which time the Faith had been established in over two hundred and fifty countries and territories, Shoghi Effendi was able to announce the purchase of property for ten new temple sites, and the commencement of work on the Houses of Worship in Kampala, Sydney and Frankfurt; the acquisition of properties for forty-six of the required national Ḥaẓíratu'l-Quds; a vast increase in the production of Bahá'í literature; additional Assembly incorporations that had raised the total number to one hundred and ninety-five; growing recognition of Bahá'í marriage and Bahá'í Holy Days; and the advancing work on the International Bahá'í Archives, the first building to be constructed on the broad arc that the Guardian had traced on the slope of Mount Carmel. No one who reviews the events of those days can fail to be deeply moved by the parental care with which Shoghi Effendi ensured the achievement of these magnificent results, as reflected in his painstaking listing by name, in the last general message he wrote on the Crusade, in April 1957, of each one of sixty-three regional teaching conferences and institutes held that year around the Bahá'í world.

Such a review would be incomplete without an understanding of parallel developments of the Administrative Order at the international level that the Guardian undertook during these years. These steps proved crucial not merely to winning the Crusade but to consolidating and protecting the future of the Cause. Alongside the decision-making authority devolved on the elective institutions of the Faith, a parallel function of the Administrative Order is to exert a spiritual, moral and intellectual influence on both these institutions and the lives of the individual members of the community. Conceived by Bahá'u'lláh Himself, this responsibility "to diffuse the Divine Fragrances, to edify the souls of men, to promote learning, to improve the character of all men…" is vested by the Master's Will and Testament particularly in the Hands of the Cause of God. [99]

During the ministries of both Bahá'u'lláh and 'Abdu'l-Bahá those believers given this high station had played crucial roles in advancing the teaching work in the Orient. As the conception of the Ten Year Crusade took shape in his mind, Shoghi Effendi moved to mobilize the spiritual support this institution could bring to achieving the tasks of the Plan. In a cablegram of 24 December 1951, he announced the appointment of the first contingent of twelve Hands of the Cause of God, allocated equally to the work in the Holy Land, in Asia, the Americas and Europe. These distinguished servants of the Cause were called upon to focus directly on the challenge of mobilizing the energies of the friends and providing the elected bodies with encouragement and counsel. Shortly thereafter the number of Hands of the Cause was raised from twelve to nineteen.

The resources available for the discharge of this responsibility were greatly increased by the Guardian's decision in October 1952, calling on the Hands of the Cause to create five auxiliary boards, one for each continent: those in the Americas, Europe and Africa consisting of nine members each, while those in Asia and Australasia having seven and two respectively. Subsequently, separate auxiliary boards were created to assist with the protection of the Faith, the other of the two chief functions of the Hands of the Cause.

A message of 3 June 1957 celebrated the action of the Israeli government in executing the final decision of the court of appeals of that country, by which the surviving band of Covenant-breakers were at last evicted from the Ḥaram-i-Aqdas surrounding the focal Centre of the Bahá'í world at Bahjí. [100] Only a day later, however, a second cablegram warned ominously of the urgent need of the Faith's senior institutions to act in concert to protect it from new dangers that the Guardian perceived to be gathering on the horizon. This was followed in October by a message announcing that the number of Hands of the Cause of God had been raised from nineteen to twenty-seven, designating these senior officers "Chief Stewards of Bahá'u'lláh's embryonic World Commonwealth", and charging them with responsibility to consult with National Spiritual Assemblies on urgently needed measures to protect the Faith.

Less than a month thereafter, the Bahá'í world was devastated by the news of Shoghi Effendi's death on 4 November 1957 from complications following an attack of Asiatic influenza contracted during the course of a visit to London. The Centre of the Cause who, for thirty-six years, had day by day guided its evolution, whose vision encompassed both the flow of events and the actions the Bahá'í community must take, and whose messages of encouragement had been the spiritual lifeline of countless Bahá'ís around the planet, was suddenly gone, leaving the great Crusade half finished and the future of the Administrative Order in crisis.

The grief and overwhelming sense of desolation produced by the loss of the Guardian lends all the greater significance to the triumph of the Plan he had conceived and inspired. On 21 April 1963, the ballots of delegates from fifty-six National Spiritual Assemblies, including the forty-four new bodies called for and successfully formed during the Ten Year Crusade, brought into existence the Universal House of Justice, the governing body of the Cause conceived by Bahá'u'lláh and assured by Him unequivocally of Divine guidance in the exercise of its functions:

> It is incumbent upon the Trustees of the House of Justice to take counsel together regarding those things which have not outwardly been revealed in the Book, and to enforce that which is agreeable to them. God will verily inspire them with whatsoever He willeth, and He, verily, is the Provider, the Omniscient.[101]

It seemed especially fitting that the election—carried out by the assembled delegates and those voting by mail—should take place in the home of the Master, whose Will and Testament had described nearly sixty years earlier the intent and scope of the authority bestowed by Bahá'u'lláh's words:

> Unto the Most Holy Book every one must turn and all that is not expressly recorded therein must be referred to the Universal House of

Justice. That which this body, whether unanimously or by a majority doth carry, that is verily the Truth and the Purpose of God Himself. Whoso doth deviate therefrom is verily of them that love discord, hath shown forth malice and turned away from the Lord of the Covenant.[102]

An important preliminary step for the election had been taken by Shoghi Effendi in 1951, in his appointment of the membership of the International Council to assist him with his work. In 1961, as he had explained would be the case, the second step in the process had been taken when this institution evolved into a nine-member Council, elected by the members of the National Spiritual Assemblies. Consequently, when the Ten Year Crusade came to its victorious end in 1963, the Bahá'í world had gained important experience in the challenging act it was then called on to perform.

Historians will unhesitatingly accord credit for mobilizing the effort that had made this moment possible to the Hands of the Cause, who provided the coordination of which the loss of the Guardian's leadership had deprived the Bahá'í world. Tirelessly coursing the earth in promotion of Shoghi Effendi's Plan, coming together in annual conclaves to provide encouragement and information, inspiring the endeavours of their newly created deputies, and fending off the efforts of a new band of Covenant-breakers to undermine the unity of the Faith, this small company of grief-stricken men and women succeeded in ensuring that the Crusade's ambitious objectives were attained in the time required and that the necessary foundation was in place for the erection of the Administrative Order's crowning unit. In asking that their own members be left free from election to the Universal House of Justice, so as to perform the services assigned them by the Guardian, the Hands also endowed the Bahá'í world, as a second great legacy, with a spiritual distinction that is without precedent in human history. Never before had persons into whose hands the supreme power in a great religion had fallen and who enjoyed a level of regard unmatched by any others in their community, requested not to be considered for participation in the exercise of supreme authority, placing themselves entirely at the service of the Body chosen by the community of their fellow believers for this role.[103]

VII

HOWEVER GREAT IS THE DISTANCE between the Guardian-ship and the unique station of the Centre of the Covenant, the role played by Shoghi Effendi after the Master's passing stands alone in the history of the Cause. It will continue to occupy this focal place in the life of the Faith throughout the coming centuries. In important respects Shoghi Effendi may be said to have extended by an additional, critical, thirty-six years the influence of the guiding hand of the Master in the building of the Administrative Order and the expansion and consolida-tion of the Faith of Bahá'u'lláh. One has only to make the fearful effort of imagining the fate of the infant Cause of God had it not been held firmly, during the period of its greatest vulnerability, in the grip of one who had been prepared for this purpose by 'Abdu'l-Bahá and who ac-cepted to serve—in the fullest sense of the word—as its Guardian.

Although emphasizing to the body of his fellow believers that the Master's twin Successors were "inseparable" and "complementary" in the functions they were individually designed to carry out, it is clear that Shoghi Effendi early accepted the implications of the fact that the Universal House of Justice could not come into existence until a lengthy process of administrative development had created the supporting

structure of National and Local Spiritual Assemblies it required. He was
entirely candid with the Bahá'í community about the implications of
the fact that he was called on to exercise his supreme responsibility
alone. In his own words:

> Severed from the no less essential institution of the Universal
> House of Justice this same System of the Will of 'Abdu'l-Bahá would
> be paralyzed in its action and would be powerless to fill in those gaps
> which the Author of the Kitáb-i-Aqdas has deliberately left in the
> body of His legislative and administrative ordinances.[104]

Aware of this truth, Shoghi Effendi proceeded with scrupulous regard
for the constraints placed on him by circumstance, a faithfulness that will
be the pride of Bahá'u'lláh's followers throughout the ages to come. The
record of his thirty-six years of service to the Faith—a record which, like
that of his Grandfather, is open for posterity to review and assess—
contains, as he assured the Bahá'í community would be the case, no action on his part that would in any degree "infringe upon the sacred and
prescribed domain" of the Universal House of Justice. It is not only that
Shoghi Effendi refrained from legislation; he was able to fulfil his mandate by introducing no more than provisional ordinances, leaving
decisions in such matters entirely to the Universal House of Justice.

Nowhere is this self-restraint more striking than in the central issue of
a successor to the Guardianship. Shoghi Effendi had no heirs of his own,
and the other branches of the Holy family had violated the Covenant.
The Bahá'í Writings contain no guidance in such an eventuality, but the
Will and Testament of the Master is explicit as to how all matters that are
unclear are to be resolved:

> It is incumbent upon these members (of the Universal House of
> Justice) to gather in a certain place and deliberate upon all problems
> which have caused difference, questions that are obscure and matters
> that are not expressly recorded in the Book. Whatsoever they decide
> has the same effect as the Text itself.[105]

In conformity with this guidance from the pen of the Centre of the
Covenant, Shoghi Effendi remained silent, leaving the question of his

successor or successors in the hands of the Body alone authorized to determine the matter. Five months after it came into existence, the Universal House of Justice clarified the issue in a message dated 6 October 1963 to all National Spiritual Assemblies:

> After prayerful and careful study of the Holy Texts ... and after prolonged consideration ... the Universal House of Justice finds that there is no way to appoint or to legislate to make it possible to appoint a second Guardian to succeed Shoghi Effendi.[106]

In embarking on a mission for which history supplied him with no precedent, Shoghi Effendi could look nowhere but to the Writings of the Founders of the Faith and the example of the Master for the guidance his work required. No body of advisors could help him determine the meaning of the Texts he was called on to interpret for a Bahá'í community that had placed its whole trust in him. Although he read widely the published works of historians, economists and political thinkers, such research could do no more than supply raw materials that his inspired vision of the Cause must then organize. The confidence and courage required in mobilizing a heterogeneous community of believers to undertake tasks that were, by any objective criteria, far beyond their capacities, could be found only in the spiritual resources of his own heart. No dispassionate observer of the twentieth century, however sceptical about the claims of religion he or she may be, can fail to acknowledge that the integrity with which a young man in his early twenties accepted so awesome a responsibility—and the magnitude of the victory he won—are evidences of an immense spiritual power inherent in the Cause he championed.

To acknowledge all this is to recognize that the capacities with which the Covenant had endowed the Guardianship were not a form of magic. Their successful exercise entailed, as Rúhíyyih Khánum has movingly described, a never-ending process of testing, evaluation, and refinement. One is awed by the precision with which Shoghi Effendi analyzed political and social processes in the early stages of their development, and the mastery with which his mind encompassed a kaleidoscope of events, both current and historical, relating their implications to the unfolding Will of Providence. That this work of the intellect was carried out on a level far above the one on which the human mind customarily operates did not make the effort any the less real or stressful. Rather, given the insight into human nature and human motivation that was an inseparable feature of the institution Shoghi Effendi represented, the opposite was the case.[107]

In the perspective of the more than forty years since Shoghi Effendi's passing, the long-term significance of his work in the evolution of the Administrative Order has begun to emerge with brilliant clarity. Had circumstances been different, the Master's Will and Testament had provided for the possibility that one or more successors might have followed in the institution Shoghi Effendi embodied. We obviously cannot penetrate the mind of God. What is clear and undeniable, however, is that, through his interpretive authority, the structure of the Administrative Order, as well as the course that its future development will pursue, have been permanently fixed by Shoghi Effendi's fulfilment—in every least respect and to the fullest extent imaginable—of the mandate laid on him by the Master. Equally clear and undeniable is the fact that both structure and course represent the Will of God.

VIII

AS SHOGHI EFFENDI HAD PROPHETICALLY WARNED, forces undermining inherited systems and convictions of every kind were continuing to advance in tandem with the integrating processes at work in the world. It is not surprising, therefore, that the euphoria induced by the restoration of peace in both Europe and the Orient proved to be of the briefest duration. Hardly had hostilities ended than the ideological divisions between Marxism and liberal democracy burst out into attempts to secure dominance between the respective blocs of nations they inspired. The phenomenon of "Cold War", in which the struggle for advantage stopped just short of military conflict, emerged as the prevailing political paradigm of the next several decades.

The threat posed by a new crisis in the international order was heightened by breakthroughs in nuclear technology and the success of both blocs of nations in equipping themselves with an ever-growing array of weapons of mass destruction. The horrific images of Hiroshima and Nagasaki had awakened humanity to the appalling possibility that a series of relatively minor mishaps, as uncalculated as the process set in motion by the 1914 incident in Sarajevo, might this time lead to the annihilation of a considerable portion of the world's population and leave large areas of the globe uninhabitable. For Bahá'ís, the prospect could only bring vividly to mind the sombre warning uttered by Bahá'u'lláh decades earlier: "Strange and astonishing things exist in the earth but they are hidden from the minds and the understanding of men. These things are capable of changing the whole atmosphere of the earth and their contamination would prove lethal."[108]

By far the greatest tragedy resulting from this latest contest for world domination was the blight that it cast over the hopes with which formerly subject peoples had welcomed the opportunity they believed they had been given to build a new life of their own devising. The obstinate determination of some of the surviving colonial powers to suppress such hopes, though doomed to failure in the eyes of any objective observer, had left the urge for liberation in many countries with no recourse but to assume the character of revolutionary struggle. By 1960, such movements, which had already been a feature of the political landscape during the earlier decades of the century, were coming to represent the principal form of indigenous political activity in most subject nations.

Since the driving force of colonialism itself was economic exploitation, it was perhaps inevitable that most movements of liberation assumed a broadly socialistic ideological cast. Within only a few short years, these circumstances had created a fertile ground for exploitation by the world's superpowers. For the Soviet Union, the situation seemed to offer an opportunity to induce a shift in the existing alignment of nations by gaining a preponderating influence in what was by now beginning to be called the "Third World". The response of the West—wherever development aid failed to retain the loyalties of recipient populations—was to resort to the encouragement and arming of a wide variety of authoritarian regimes.

As outside forces manipulated new governments, attention was increasingly diverted from an objective consideration of developmental needs to ideological and political struggles that bore little or no relation to social or economic reality. The results were uniformly devastating. Economic bankruptcy, gross violations of human rights, the breakdown of civil administration and the rise of opportunistic elites who saw in the suffering of their countries only openings for self-enrichment—such was the heartbreaking fate that engulfed one after another of the new nations who, only short years before, had begun life with such great promise.

Inspiring these political, social and economic crises was the inexorable rise and consolidation of a disease of the human soul infinitely more destructive than any of its specific manifestations. Its triumph marked a new and ominous stage in the process of social and spiritual degeneration that Shoghi Effendi had identified. Fathered by nineteenth century European thought, acquiring enormous influence through the achievements of American capitalist culture, and endowed by Marxism with the counterfeit credibility peculiar to that system, materialism emerged full-blown in the second half of the twentieth century as a kind of universal religion claiming absolute authority in both the personal and social life of humankind. Its creed was simplicity itself. Reality—including human reality and the process by which it evolves—is essentially material in nature. The goal of human life is, or ought to be, the satisfaction of material needs and wants. Society exists to facilitate this quest, and the collective concern of humankind should be an ongoing refinement of the system, aimed at rendering it ever more efficient in carrying out its assigned task.

With the collapse of the Soviet Union, impulses to devise and promote any formal materialistic belief system disappeared. Nor would any useful purpose have been served by such efforts, as materialism was soon facing no significant challenge in most parts of the world. Religion, where not simply driven back into fanaticism and unthinking rejection of progress, became progressively reduced to a kind of personal preference, a predilection, a pursuit designed to satisfy spiritual and emotional needs of the individual. The sense of historical mission that had defined the major Faiths learned to content itself with providing religious endorsement for campaigns of social change carried on by secular movements. The academic world, once the scene of great exploits of the mind and spirit, settled into the role of a kind of scholastic industry preoccupied with tending its machinery of dissertations, symposia, publication credits and grants.

Whether as world-view or simple appetite, materialism's effect is to leach out of human motivation—and even interest—the spiritual

impulses that distinguish the rational soul. "For self-love," 'Abdu'l-Bahá
has said, "is kneaded into the very clay of man, and it is not possible that,
without any hope of a substantial reward, he should neglect his own
present material good."[109] In the absence of conviction about the spiritual nature of reality and the fulfilment it alone offers, it is not surprising
to find at the very heart of the current crisis of civilization a cult of indi-
vidualism that increasingly admits of no restraint and that elevates
acquisition and personal advancement to the status of major cultural
values. The resulting atomization of society has marked a new stage in the
process of disintegration about which the writings of Shoghi Effendi
speak so urgently.

To accept willingly the rupture of one after another strand of the
moral fabric that guides and disciplines individual life in any social system, is a self-defeating approach to reality. If leaders of thought were to
be candid in their assessment of the evidence readily available, it is here
that one would find the root cause of such apparently unrelated problems
as the pollution of the environment, economic dislocation, ethnic violence, spreading public apathy, the massive increase in crime, and
epidemics that ravage whole populations. However important the application of legal, sociological or technological expertise to such issues
undoubtedly is, it would be unrealistic to imagine that efforts of this kind
will produce any significant recovery without a fundamental change of
moral consciousness and behaviour.

What the Bahá'í world accomplished during those same years ac-
quires an added brilliancy against the background of this darkened
horizon. It is impossible to exaggerate the significance of the achievement
that brought the Universal House of Justice into existence. For some six
thousand years humanity has experimented with an almost unlimited
variety of methods for collective decision-making. From the vantage
point of the twentieth century, the political history of the world presents
a constantly shifting scene in which there was no possibility that was not

seized upon by human ingenuity. Systems based on principles as different as theocracy, monarchy, aristocracy, oligarchy, republic, democracy and near anarchy have proliferated freely, along with innovations without end that have sought to combine various desirable features of these possibilities. Although most of the options have lent themselves to abuses of one kind or another, the great majority have no doubt contributed in varying degrees to fulfilling hopes of those whose interests they purportedly served.

During this long evolutionary process, as ever larger and more diverse populations came under the control of one or another system of government, the temptation of universal empire repeatedly seized the imaginations of the Caesars and Napoleons directing such expansion. The resulting series of calamitous failures that have lent history so much of its ability to both fascinate and appal, would seem to provide persuasive evidence that the realization of the ambition lies beyond the reach of any human agency, no matter how great the resources available to it or how firm its confidence in the genius of its particular culture.

Yet, the unification of humankind under a system of governance that can release the full potentialities latent in human nature, and allow their expression in programmes for the benefit of all, is clearly the next stage in the evolution of civilization. The physical unification of the planet in our time and the awakening aspirations of the mass of its inhabitants have at last produced the conditions that permit achievement of the ideal, although in a manner far different from that imagined by imperial dreamers of the past. To this effort the governments of the world have contributed the founding of the United Nations Organization, with all its great blessings, all its regrettable shortcomings.

Somewhere ahead lie the further great changes that will eventually impel acceptance of the principle of world government itself. The United Nations does not possess such a mandate, nor is there anything in the current discourse of political leaders that seriously envisions so radical a restructuring of the administration of the affairs of the planet. That it will come about in due course Bahá'u'lláh has made unmistakably clear. That yet greater suffering and disillusionment will be required to impel humanity to this great leap forward appears, alas, equally clear. Its establishment will require national governments and other centres of power to surrender

to international determination, unconditionally and irreversibly, the full
measure of overriding authority implicit in the word "government".

This is the context in which Bahá'ís must strive to appreciate the
unique victory that the Cause won in 1963, and which has consolidated
itself over the years since then. A full understanding of its meaning is
beyond the reach of the present and perhaps of the next several generations
of believers. To the extent that a Bahá'í does grasp it, he or she will hold
nothing back in a determination to serve its unfolding purpose.

The process leading to the election of the Universal House of
Justice—made possible by the successful completion of the three initial
stages of the Master's Divine Plan under the leadership of Shoghi Effendi
—very likely constituted history's first global democratic election. Each
of the successive elections since then has been carried out by an ever
broader and more diverse body of the community's chosen delegates, a
development that has now reached the point that it incontestably represents the will of a cross-section of the entire human race. There is nothing
in existence—nothing indeed envisioned by any group of people —that
in any way resembles this achievement.

When one considers, further, the spiritual atmosphere that pervades
Bahá'í elections and the principled conduct called for in even their simplest operations, one is humbled by a much greater awareness. In the
raising up of the supreme governing institution of our Faith, one is witnessing a striving to the utmost of human capacity to win the good
pleasure of God, a united and ardent determination that nothing whatever, in either cultural conditioning or the promptings of personal
desire, should be allowed to stain the purity of this ultimate collective
act. Nothing beyond this lies within human power. By its action, humanity has done literally everything of which it is capable, and God, in
accepting this consecrated effort on the part of those who have embraced His Cause, endows the institution thus brought into existence
with those powers promised to it in the Kitáb-i-Aqdas and the Will and
Testament of 'Abdu'l-Bahá. Little wonder that 'Abdu'l-Bahá foresaw in
the process leading up to the culminating historical moment reached in
1963, the centenary of Bahá'u'lláh's declaration of His mission, the fulfilment of the vision of the prophet Daniel, "Blessed is he that waiteth

and cometh unto the thousand, three hundred and five and thirty days." In the Master's words:

> For according to this calculation a century will have elapsed from the dawn of the Sun of Truth, then will the teachings of God be firmly established upon the earth, and the Divine Light shall flood the world from the East even unto the West. Then, on this day, will the faithful rejoice![110]

With the establishment of the Universal House of Justice, the second of the two successor institutions named by 'Abdu'l-Bahá as the guarantors of the integrity of the Cause had emerged. The vast body of the Guardian's writings and the pattern of administrative life he had created and which were imprinted indelibly in Bahá'í consciousness, had endowed the Bahá'í world with the means to ensure universal agreement about the intent of the Revelation of God. In the Universal House of Justice it now also possessed the ultimate authority conceived by Bahá'u'lláh for the exercise of the decision-making functions of the Administrative Order. As the Will and Testament explains, the two institutions share jointly in the Divine promise of unfailing guidance:

> The sacred and youthful branch, the guardian of the Cause of God as well as the Universal House of Justice, to be universally elected and established, are both under the care and protection of the Abhá Beauty, under the shelter and unerring guidance of His Holiness, the Exalted One (may my life be offered up for them both). Whatsoever they decide is of God.[111]

The relationship between these two centres of authority, Shoghi Effendi further explained, is a complementary one, in which some functions are shared in common and others specialized for one or other of the two institutions. Nevertheless, he was at pains to emphasize:

> It must be ... clearly understood by every believer that the institution of Guardianship does not under any circumstances abrogate, or even in the slightest degree detract from, the powers granted to the Universal House of Justice by Bahá'u'lláh in the Kitáb-i-Aqdas, and

repeatedly and solemnly confirmed by 'Abdu'l-Bahá in His Will. It does not constitute in any manner a contradiction to the Will and Writings of Bahá'u'lláh, nor does it nullify any of His revealed instructions.[112]

Realization of the uniqueness of what Bahá'u'lláh has brought into being opens the imagination to the contribution that the Cause can make to the unification of humankind and the building of a global society. The immediate responsibility of establishing world government rests on the shoulders of the nation-states. What the Bahá'í community is called on to do, at this stage in humanity's social and political evolution, is to contribute by every means in its power to the creation of conditions that will encourage and facilitate this enormously demanding undertaking. In the same way that Bahá'u'lláh assured the monarchs of His day that "It is not Our wish to lay hands on your kingdoms",[113] so the Bahá'í community has no political agenda, abstains from all involvement in partisan activity, and accepts unreservedly the authority of civil government in public affairs. Whatever concern Bahá'ís may have about current conditions or about the needs of their own members is expressed through constitutional channels.

The power that the Cause possesses to influence the course of history thus lies not only in the spiritual potency of its message but in the example it provides. "So powerful is the light of unity," Bahá'u'lláh asserts, "that it can illuminate the whole earth."[114] The oneness of humankind embodied in the Faith represents, as Shoghi Effendi emphasized, "no mere outburst of ignorant emotionalism or an expression of vague and pious hope". The organic unity of the body of believers—and the Administrative Order that makes it possible—are evidences of what Shoghi Effendi termed "the society-building power which their Faith possesses."[115] As the Cause expands and the capacities latent in its Administrative Order become ever more apparent, it will increasingly attract the attention of leaders of thought, inspiring progressive minds with confidence that their ideals are ultimately attainable. In Shoghi Effendi's words:

> Leaders of religion, exponents of political theories, governors of human institutions, who at present are witnessing with perplexity and

dismay the bankruptcy of their ideas, and the disintegration of their handiwork, would do well to turn their gaze to the Revelation of Bahá'u'lláh, and to meditate upon the World Order which, lying enshrined in His teachings, is slowly and imperceptibly rising amid the welter and chaos of present-day civilization.[116]

Such an examination will focus attention on the power that has made it possible for Bahá'í unity to be achieved, consolidated and maintained. "The light of men," Bahá'u'lláh says, "is Justice." Its purpose, He adds, "is the appearance of unity among men. The ocean of divine wisdom surgeth within this exalted word".[117] The designation "Houses of Justice" given to the institutions that will govern the World Order He conceived, at local, national and international levels, reflects the centrality of this principle in the teachings of the Revelation and the life of the Cause. As the Bahá'í community becomes an increasingly familiar participant in the life of society, its experience will offer ever more encouraging evidence of this crucial law in healing the countless ills which, in the final analysis, are the consequences of the disunity afflicting the human family. "Know thou, of a truth," Bahá'u'lláh explains, "these great oppressions that have befallen the world are preparing it for the advent of the Most Great Justice."[118] Clearly, that culminating stage in the evolution of human society will take place in a world very different from the one we know today.

IX

THE IMMEDIATE EFFECT of the winning of the Ten Year Crusade and the establishment of the Universal House of Justice was to give a powerful impetus to the advance of the Cause. This time the progress—which affected virtually every aspect of Bahá'í life—took the form of long-range developments that are best appreciated when the entire period since 1963 is viewed as a whole. During these crucial thirty-seven years the work proceeded rapidly forward along two parallel tracks: the expansion and consolidation of the Bahá'í community itself and, along with it, a dramatic rise in the influence the Faith came to exercise in the life of society. While the range of Bahá'í activities greatly diversified, most such efforts tended to contribute directly to one or other of the two main developments.

A decision taken by the House of Justice at an early point in the period proved crucial to all aspects of both teaching and administrative development. Realization that there was no successor to Shoghi Effendi brought with it recognition that neither would the appointment of new Hands of the Cause be any longer possible. How essential the functions of this institution are to the progress of the Faith had been demonstrated with unforgettable force during the anxious six years between 1957 and 1963. Accordingly, in pursuance of the mandate authorizing it to bring into existence new Bahá'í institutions,[119] as the needs of the Cause require, the House of Justice created, in June 1968, the Continental Boards of Counsellors. Empowered to extend into the future the functions of the Hands of the Cause for the protection and propagation of the Faith, the new institution assumed responsibility for guiding the work of the already existing Auxiliary Boards and joined National Assemblies in shouldering responsibilities for the advancement of the Faith. The great victories celebrated at the end of the Nine Year Plan in 1973, splendid in themselves, reflected the extraordinary ease with which the new administrative agency had taken up its duties and the eagerness with which it had been welcomed by believers and Assemblies alike. The moment was marked by another major development of the Administrative Order, the creation of the International Teaching Centre, the Body that would carry into the future certain of the responsibilities performed by the group of "Hands of the Cause Residing in the Holy Land", and from this point on coordinate the work of the Boards of Counsellors around the world.

Envisioning the course that the growth of the Cause would follow, Shoghi Effendi had written of "the launching of worldwide enterprises destined to be embarked upon, in future epochs of that same [Formative] Age, by the Universal House of Justice, that will symbolize the unity and coordinate and unify the activities of … National Assemblies."[120] These global undertakings began in 1964 with the Nine Year Plan, to be followed by a Five Year Plan (1974), a Seven Year Plan (1979), a Six Year Plan (1986), a Three Year Plan (1993), a Four Year Plan (1996), and a Twelve Month Plan that ended the century. The shifts in emphasis that distinguished these successive endeavours from one another provide a useful index to the growth that the Cause was experiencing in these decades and the new opportunities and challenges that this growth produced. Far more important than the differences amongst them, however, is the fact that the activities called for in each Plan were extensions of initiatives which had been set in motion by Shoghi Effendi, who in turn had seized up and elaborated strands woven by the Faith's Founders—the training of Spiritual Assemblies; the translation, production and distribution of literature; the encouragement of universal participation by the friends; attention to the spiritual enrichment of

Bahá'í life; efforts toward the involvement of the Bahá'í community in the life of society; the strengthening of Bahá'í family life; and the education of children and youth. While these various processes will continue indefinitely to unfold new possibilities, the fact that each originated in the creative impulse of the Revelation itself lends to everything the Bahá'í community does a unifying force that is both the secret and the guarantee of its ultimate success.

The first two decades of the process were one of the most enriching periods that the Bahá'í community has experienced. Within a remarkably short period of time, the number of Local Spiritual Assemblies multiplied and the ethnic and cultural diversity of the membership became an ever more distinctive feature of Bahá'í life. Although the breakdown of society was creating problems for Bahá'í administrative institutions, a related effect was to generate a greatly increased interest in the message of the Cause. At the outset, the community was introduced to the challenge of "teaching the masses". By 1967, it was being called on "to launch, on a global scale and to every stratum of human society, an enduring and intensive proclamation of the healing message that the Promised One has come...."[121]

As believers from urban centres set out on sustained campaigns to reach the mass of the world's peoples living in villages and rural areas, they encountered a receptivity to Bahá'u'lláh's message far beyond anything they had imagined possible. While the response usually took forms very different from the ones with which the teachers had been familiar, the new declarants were eagerly welcomed. Tens of thousands of new Bahá'ís poured into the Cause throughout Africa, Asia and Latin America, often representing the greater part of whole rural villages. The 1960s and 1970s were heady days for a Bahá'í community most of whose growth outside of Iran had been slow and measured. To the friends in the Pacific went the great distinction of attracting into the Cause the first Head of State, His Highness Malietoa Tanumafili II of Samoa, a distinction for which only future events will provide an adequate frame.

At the heart of the development, as has been the case in the life of the Cause from the outset, was the commitment made by the individual believer. Already, during the ministry of Shoghi Effendi, far-sighted persons had taken the initiative to reach indigenous populations in such countries as Uganda, Bolivia and Indonesia. During the Nine Year Plan, ever larger numbers of such teachers were drawn into the work, particularly in India, several countries in Africa, and most regions of Latin America, as well as in islands of the Pacific, Alaska and among the native peoples of Canada and the rural black population of the southern United States. Pioneering brought vital support to the work, encouraging the emergence of groups of teachers among the indigenous believers themselves.

Even so, it soon became apparent that individual initiative alone, however inspired and energetic, could not respond adequately to the opportunities opening up. The result was to launch Bahá'í communities on a wide range of collective teaching and proclamation projects recalling the heroic days of the dawn-breakers. Teams of ardent teachers found that it was now possible to introduce the message of the Faith not merely to a succession of inquirers, but to entire groups and even whole communities. The tens of thousands became hundreds of thousands. The Faith's growth meant that members of Spiritual Assemblies, whose experience had been limited to confirming the understanding of the Faith of individual applicants raised in cultures of doubt or religious fanaticism, had to adjust to expressions of belief on the part of whole groups of people to whom religious awareness and response were normal features of daily life.

No segment of the community made a more energetic or significant contribution to this dramatic process of growth than did Bahá'í youth. In their exploits during these crucial decades—as, indeed, throughout the entire history of the past one hundred and fifty years—one is reminded again and again that the great majority of the band of heroes who launched the Cause on its course in the middle years of the nineteenth century were all of them young people. The Báb Himself declared His mission when He was twenty-five years old, and Anís, who attained the imperishable glory of dying with his Lord, was only a youth. Quddús responded to the Revelation at the age of twenty-two. Zaynab, whose age was never recorded, was a very young woman. Shaykh 'Alí, so greatly cherished by both Quddús and Mullá Ḥusayn, was martyred at the age of twenty, while Muḥammad-i-Báqir-Naqsh laid down his life when he was only fourteen. Ṭáhirih was in her twenties when she embraced the Báb's Cause.

Following in the path that these extraordinary figures had opened, thousands of young Bahá'ís arose in subsequent years to proclaim the message of the Faith throughout all five continents and the scattered islands of the globe. As an international youth culture began to emerge in society during the late nineteen sixties and seventies, believers with talent in music, drama and the arts demonstrated something of what Shoghi Effendi had meant when he pointed out: "That day will the Cause spread like wildfire when its spirit and teachings are presented on the stage or in art and literature...."[122] The spirit of zeal and enthusiasm characteristic of youth has also provided an ongoing challenge to the general body of the community to explore ever more audaciously the revolutionary social implications of Bahá'u'lláh's teachings.

The burst of enrolments brought with it, however, equally great problems. At the immediate level, the resources of Bahá'í communities engaged in the work were soon overwhelmed by the task of providing the sustained deepening the masses of new believers needed and the consolidation of the resulting communities and Spiritual Assemblies. Beyond that, cultural challenges like those encountered by the early Persian believers who had first sought to introduce the Faith in Western lands now replicated themselves throughout the world. Theological and administrative principles that might be of consuming interest to pioneers and teachers were seldom those that were central to the concern of new declarants from very different social and cultural backgrounds. Often, differences of view about even such elementary matters as the use of time or simple social conventions created gaps of understanding that made communication extremely difficult.

Initially, such problems proved stimulating as both Bahá'í institutions and individual believers struggled to find new ways of looking at situations—new ways, indeed, of understanding important passages in the Bahá'í Writings themselves. Determined efforts were made to respond to the guidance of the World Centre that expansion and consolidation are twin processes that must go hand in hand. Where hoped for results did not readily materialize, however, a measure of discouragement frequently set in. The initial rapid rise in enrolment rates slowed markedly in many countries, tempting some Bahá'í institutions and communities to turn back to more familiar activities and more accessible publics.

The principal effect of the setbacks, however, was that they brought home to communities that the high expectations of the early years were in some respects quite unrealistic. Although the easy successes of the initial teaching activities were encouraging, they did not, by themselves, build a Bahá'í community life that could meet the needs of its new members and be self-generating. Rather, pioneers and new believers alike faced questions for which Bahá'í experience in Western lands—or even Iran—offered few answers. How were Local Spiritual Assemblies to be established—and once established, how were they to function—in areas where large numbers of new believers had joined the Cause overnight, simply on the strength of their spiritual apprehension of its truth? How, in societies dominated by men since the dawn of time, were women to be accorded an equal voice? How was the education of large numbers of children to be systematically addressed in cultural situations where poverty and illiteracy prevailed? What priorities should guide Bahá'í moral teaching, and how could these objectives best be related to prevailing indigenous conventions? How could a vibrant community life be cultivated that would stimulate the spiritual growth of its members? What priorities, too, should be set with respect to the production of Bahá'í literature, particularly given the sudden explosion that had taken place in the number of languages represented in the community? How could the integrity of the Bahá'í institution of the Nineteen Day Feast be maintained, while opening this vital activity to the enriching influence of diverse cultures? And, in all areas of concern, how were the necessary resources to be recruited, funded, and coordinated?

The pressure of these urgent and interlocking challenges launched the Bahá'í world on a learning process that has proved to be as important as the expansion itself. It is safe to say that during these years there was virtually no type of teaching activity, no combination of expansion, consolidation and proclamation, no administrative option, no effort at cultural adaptation that was not being energetically tried in some part of the Bahá'í world. The net result of the experience was an intensive education of a great part of the Bahá'í community in the implications of the mass teaching work, an education that could have occurred in no other way. By its very nature, the process was largely local and regional in focus, qualitative rather than quantitative in its gains, and incremental rather than large-scale in the progress achieved. Had it not been for the painstaking, always difficult and often frustrating consolidation work pursued during these years, however, the subsequent strategy of systematizing the promotion of entry by troops would have had very little with which to work.

The fact that the Bahá'í message was now penetrating the lives not merely of small groups of individuals but of whole communities also had the effect of reviving a vital feature of an earlier stage in the advancement of the Cause. For the first time in decades, the Faith found itself once more in a situation where teaching and consolidation were inseparably bound up with social and economic development. In the early years of the century, under the guidance of the Master and the Guardian, the Iranian believers—denied the opportunity to participate equally in whatever limited benefits the society of the day offered—had arisen to painstakingly construct a comprehensive community life of a kind beyond either the need or the reach of the relatively isolated Bahá'í groups across North America and Western Europe. In Iran, spiritual and moral advancement, teaching activities, the creation of schools and clinics, the building of administrative institutions, and the encouragement of initiatives aimed at economic self-sufficiency and prosperity—all had been from an early stage inseparable features of one organically unified process of development. Now—in Africa, in Latin America, and parts of Asia —the same challenges and opportunities had re-emerged.

While social and economic development activities had long been under way, particularly in Latin America and Asia, these had been isolated projects carried out by groups of believers under the guidance of individual National Assemblies, and unrelated to any plan. In October 1983, however, Bahá'í communities throughout the world were called on to begin incorporating such efforts into their regular programmes of work. An Office of Social and Economic Development was created at the World Centre to coordinate learning and help seek financial support.

The decade that followed saw wide experimentation in a field of work for which most Bahá'í institutions had little preparation. While striving to benefit from the models being tried by the many development agencies operating around the world, Bahá'í communities faced the challenge of relating what they found in various areas of concern—education, health, literacy, agriculture and communications technology—to their understanding of Bahá'í principles. The temptation was great, given the magnitude of the resources being invested by governments and foundations, and the confidence with which this effort was pursued, merely to borrow methods current at the moment or to adapt Bahá'í efforts to prevailing theories. As the work evolved, however, Bahá'í institutions began turning their attention to the goal of devising development paradigms that could assimilate what they were observing in the larger society to the Faith's unique conception of human potentialities.

Nowhere was the strategy of the successive Plans so impressively vindicated as was the case in India. The community there has today become a giant of the Cause, numbering well over a million souls. Its work stretches across the expanse of a vast sub-continent, home to an immense diversity of cultures, languages, ethnic groups and religious traditions. In many respects, the experience of this greatly blessed body of believers encapsulates the Bahá'í world's struggles, experiments, setbacks and victories throughout these critical three decades. The dramatic rise in enrolments had brought with it all of the problems being encountered elsewhere in the world, but on a massive scale. The long road leading the Indian Bahá'í community to its present-day eminence was beset with the most painful difficulties, some of which threatened at times to overwhelm the administrative resources available. The victories won, however, provide a foretaste of the confirmations that will in time bless the efforts of Bahá'í communities struggling with the same challenges on other continents. By 1985, the growth of the Faith in India had reached the point where the needs and opportunities of so many diverse regions called for more sharply focused attention than the National Spiritual Assembly alone could provide. Thus was born the new institution of the Regional Bahá'í Council, setting in motion the process of administrative decentralization that has since proven so effective in many other lands.

In 1986, the expansion and consolidation taking place in India were befittingly crowned with the inauguration of the beautiful "Lotus Temple". Although the project had raised optimistic expectations as to the impact its completion would have on public recognition of the Faith, the reality has infinitely surpassed the brightest of such hopes. Today, India's House of Worship has become the foremost visitors' attraction on the subcontinent, welcoming an average of over ten thousand visitors every day, and featuring prominently in publications, films and television productions. The interest aroused in a Faith that could inspire and embody itself in so magnificent a creation has given new meaning to the description by 'Abdu'l-Bahá of Bahá'í Temples as "silent teachers" of the Faith.

The progress of the Indian Bahá'í community, both in its internal development and its relationship with the larger society, was illustrated by a pioneering initiative undertaken in November 2000 in the field of social and economic development. Taking advantage of the reputation it had deservedly won among progressive circles in the country, the National Spiritual Assembly hosted, in collaboration with the Bahá'í International Community's newly created Institute for Studies in Global Prosperity,[123] a symposium on the subject of "Science, Religion and Development". The project engaged the participation of over one hundred of the most influential development organizations in the country and inspired national media coverage. Marking out a distinctive Bahá'í contribution to the promotion of social advancement, the event set the stage for symposia of the same kind in Africa, Latin America and other regions, where creative Bahá'í communities can help shape what may well become one of the Faith's major success stories.

During these same years, the Asian continent also saw the sudden emergence of the Malaysian Bahá'í community as an engine of the expansion work, winning its own goals with stunning speed and dispatching pioneers and travelling teachers to neighbouring lands. A development that made this dramatic advance possible was the bonds of spiritual partnership that had been woven between believers of Chinese and Indian backgrounds. Visitors to Malaysia spoke, with something approaching awe, of the way in which the Malaysian community, although working under many constraints and disabilities, seemed to be the very embodiment of the military metaphors with which Shoghi Effendi's writings seek to capture the spirit of Bahá'í teaching efforts.

Neither the world-wide growth of the Bahá'í community nor the process of learning it was experiencing, however, tell the whole story of these tumultuous and creative decades. When the history of the period is eventually written, one of its most brilliant chapters will recount the spiritual victories won by Bahá'í communities, in Africa particularly, who survived war, terror, political oppression and extreme privations, and who emerged from these tests with their faith intact, determined to resume the interrupted work of building a viable Bahá'í collective life. The community in Ethiopia, homeland of one of the world's oldest and richest cultural traditions, succeeded in maintaining both the morale of its members and the coherence of its administrative structures under relentless pressure from a brutal dictatorship. Of the friends in other countries on the continent, it may be truly said that their path of faithfulness to the Cause led through a hell of suffering seldom equalled in modern history. The annals of the Faith possess few more moving testimonies to the sheer power of the spirit than the stories of courage and purity of heart emerging from the inferno that engulfed the friends in what was then Zaire, stories that will inspire generations to come and represent priceless contributions to the creation of a global Bahá'í culture. Such countries as Uganda and Rwanda added unforgettable achievements of their own to this record of heroic struggle.

Inspiring, too, was the demonstration of the capacity for renewal that is inherent in the Cause and which emerged in Cambodian refugee camps along the Thailand border. Through the heroic efforts of a handful of teachers, Local Spiritual Assemblies were established among people who had survived a campaign of genocide almost beyond the capacity of the human heart to contemplate, who had lost countless loved ones as well as everything they possessed in the way of material security, but in whom still burned the longing of the human soul for spiritual truth. An extraordinary achievement of a related kind was that of the Liberian Bahá'í community. Driven from their homes into exile in neighbouring lands, many of these intrepid believers transported with them their whole community life, setting up Local Spiritual Assemblies, carrying on teaching work, continuing the education of their children, using their time to learn new skills, and finding in music, dance and drama powers of the spirit that helped keep hope alive until they could return to their country.

As the process of education in methods of mass teaching was taking place, the Faith's membership was being transformed. In 1992, the Bahá'í world celebrated its second Holy Year, this one marking the centenary of the ascension of Bahá'u'lláh and the promulgation of His Covenant. More eloquently than words could have done, the ethnic, cultural and national diversity of the 27,000 believers who gathered at the Javits Convention Center in New York City—together with the thousands present at nine auxiliary conferences in Bucharest, Buenos Aires, Moscow, Nairobi, New Delhi, Panama City, Singapore, Sydney and Western Samoa—provided compelling evidence of the success of Bahá'í teaching work around the world. An affecting moment occurred when the network of satellite broadcasts linked the gathering in Moscow with the one taking place in New York City, and Bahá'ís everywhere thrilled to greetings in Russian—the common language of some 280 million people from at least fifteen countries—that proclaimed a new phase in humanity's response to Bahá'u'lláh.

In the Moscow and Bucharest conferences could be glimpsed the rebirth of Bahá'í communities that had been nearly extinguished under the oppression of the Soviet regime and its collaborators. One of the last three surviving Hands of the Cause, 'Alí-Akbar Furútan, who had lived in Russia, had the great joy of returning to Moscow, at the age of eighty-six, for the inaugural election of the National Assembly of that country. Local Spiritual Assemblies sprang up in all of the newly opened lands, and six new National Spiritual Assemblies were elected. In a brief space of time, pioneering and teaching activities in countries along the southern rim of the former Soviet empire—where the Faith had been similarly proscribed —soon brought into existence still more Local Assemblies and eight additional National Spiritual Assemblies. Bahá'í literature was translated into a range of new languages, energetic steps were taken to secure civil recognition of Bahá'í institutions, and representatives from Eastern Europe and the countries of the now vanished Soviet bloc began participating with their fellow believers in the external affairs work of the Faith at the international level.

Gradually, too, the message of the Faith began to find a welcome in many parts of China and among Chinese populations abroad. Bahá'í literature was translated into Mandarin, university audiences in many Chinese cities extended invitations to Bahá'í scholars, a Centre for Bahá'í Studies was established at the prestigious Institute of World Religions in Beijing,[124] which operates within the Academy of Social Sciences, and many Chinese dignitaries have been generous in their appreciation of the principles they discover in the Writings. In light of the high praise of the Master for Chinese civilization and its role in humanity's future, one begins to anticipate the creative contribution that believers from this background will make to the intellectual and moral life of the Cause in the years ahead.[125]

The significance of these three decades of struggle, learning and sacrifice became apparent when the moment arrived to devise a global Plan that would capitalize on the insights gained and the resources that had been developed. The Bahá'í community that set out on the Four Year Plan in 1996 was a very different one from the eager, but new and still inexperienced body of believers who, in 1964, had ventured out on the first of such undertakings that were no longer sustained by the guiding hand of Shoghi Effendi. By 1996, it had become possible to see all of the distinct strands of the enterprise as integral parts of one coherent whole.

With this education had also come a much needed perspective on what had been accomplished. The expansion of the Cause over the preceding three decades had represented the response of several million human beings who had been affected by their encounter with the message of Bahá'u'lláh to the point that they were moved to identify themselves in varying degrees with the Cause of God. They were aware that a new Messenger of the Divine had appeared, had caught something of the spirit of faith, and had been strongly affected by the Bahá'í teaching of the oneness of humankind. A small minority among them were able to go beyond this point. For the most part, however, these friends were essentially recipients of teaching programmes conducted by teachers and pioneers from outside. One of the great strengths of the masses of humankind from among whom the newly enrolled believers came lies in an openness of heart that has the potentiality to generate lasting social transformation. The greatest handicap of these same populations has so far been a passivity learned through generations of exposure to outside influences which, no matter how great their material advantages, have pursued agendas that were often related only tangentially—if at all—to the realities of the needs and daily lives of indigenous peoples.

The Four Year Plan, which was a major advance on those that immediately preceded it, was designed to take advantage of the opportunities and insights thus offered. The goal of advancing the process of entry by troops became the single-minded aim of the enterprise. The lessons that had been learned during earlier Plans now placed the emphasis on developing the capacities of believers—wherever they might be—so that all could arise as confident protagonists of the Faith's mission. The instrument to accomplish this objective had been undergoing steady refinement during the earlier Plans and had demonstrated its efficacy.

As with most of the other methods and activities by which the Faith was advancing, this instrument had likewise been conceived decades earlier by the Master, who calls in the Tablets of the Divine Plan for deepened believers to "gather together the youths of the love of God in schools of instruction and teach them all the divine proofs and irrefragable arguments, explain and elucidate the history of the Cause, and interpret also the prophecies and proofs which are recorded and are extant in the divine books and epistles regarding the manifestation of the Promised One...."[126] Pioneering work and organized training of this nature had already been done in Iran, during the early years of the century, by the much-loved Ṣadru'ṣ-Ṣudúr.[127] As the years passed, winter and summer schools had multiplied, and successive Plans also encouraged experimentation in the development of Bahá'í institutes.

By far the most significant advance in this latter respect occurred over a period of more than two decades, beginning in the 1970s in Colombia, where a systematic and sustained programme of education in the Writings was devised and soon adopted in neighbouring countries. Influenced by the Colombian community's parallel efforts in the field of social and economic development, the breakthrough was all the more impressive in the fact that it was achieved against a background of violence and lawlessness that was deranging the life of the surrounding society.

The Colombian achievement proved a source of great inspiration and example to Bahá'í communities elsewhere in the world. By the time the Four Year Plan ended, over one hundred thousand believers were involved world-wide in the programmes of the more than three hundred permanent training institutes. In accomplishing this goal, a majority of regional institutes had carried the process a stage further by creating networks of "study circles" which utilize the talents of believers to replicate the work of the institute at a local level. It is already apparent that the success of the institute work has significantly reinforced the long-term process by which a universal system of Bahá'í education will take shape.[128]

Although the struggles of these decades were relatively modest—at least when set against the standard of the Heroic Age—they provide the present generation of Bahá'ís with a window on what Shoghi Effendi describes as the cyclical nature of the Faith's history: "a series of internal and external crises, of varying severity, devastating in their immediate effects, but each mysteriously releasing a corresponding measure of divine power, lending thereby a fresh impulse to its unfoldment."[129] These words put into perspective the succession of efforts, experiments, heartbreaks and victories that characterized the beginning of large-scale teaching, and prepared the Bahá'í community for the much greater challenges ahead.

Throughout history, the masses of humanity have been, at best, spectators at the advance of civilization. Their role has been to serve the designs of whatever elite had temporarily assumed control of the process. Even the successive Revelations of the Divine, whose objective was the liberation of the human spirit, were, in time, taken captive by "the insistent self", were frozen into man-made dogma, ritual, clerical privilege and sectarian quarrels, and reached their end with their ultimate purpose frustrated.

Bahá'u'lláh has come to free humanity from this long bondage, and the closing decades of the twentieth century were devoted by the community of His followers to creative experimentation with the means by which His objective can be realized. The prosecution of the Divine Plan entails no less than the involvement of the entire body of humankind in the work of its own spiritual, social and intellectual development. The trials encountered by the Bahá'í community in the decades since 1963 are those necessary ones that refine endeavour and purify motivation so as to render those who would take part worthy of so great a trust. Such tests are the surest evidences of that process of maturation which 'Abdu'l-Bahá so confidently described:

> Some movements appear, manifest a brief period of activity, then discontinue. Others show forth a greater measure of growth and strength, but before attaining mature development, weaken, disintegrate and are lost in oblivion.... There is still another kind of movement or cause which from a very small, inconspicuous beginning goes forward with sure and steady progress, gradually broadening and widening until it has assumed universal dimensions. The Bahá'í Movement is of this nature.[130]

X

BAHÁ'U'LLÁH'S MISSION IS NOT LIMITED to the building of
the Bahá'í community. The Revelation of God has come for the whole
of humanity, and it will win the support of the institutions of society to
the extent that they find in its example encouragement and inspiration
for their efforts to lay the foundations of a just society. To appreciate the
importance of this parallel concern, one has only to recall the time and
care that Bahá'u'lláh Himself devoted to cultivating relationships with
government officials, leaders of thought, prominent figures in various
minority groups, and the diplomatic representatives of foreign governments assigned to service in the Ottoman empire. The spiritual effect of
this effort is apparent in the tributes paid to His character and principles
by even such bitter enemies as 'Álí Páshá and the Persian ambassador to
Constantinople, Mírzá Ḥusayn Khán. The former, who condemned his
Prisoner to banishment in the penal colony at 'Akká, was nevertheless
moved to describe Him as "a man of great distinction, exemplary conduct, great moderation, and a most dignified figure", whose teachings
were, in the minister's opinion "worthy of high esteem".[131] The latter,
whose machinations had been principally responsible for poisoning the
minds of 'Álí Páshá and his colleagues, frankly admitted, in later years,

the great contrast between the moral and intellectual stature of his Enemy and the harm done to Persian-Turkish relations by the reputation for greed and dishonesty that characterized most of his other countrymen resident in Constantinople.

From the beginning, 'Abdu'l-Bahá took keen interest in efforts to bring into existence a new international order. It is significant, for example, that His early public references in North America to the purpose of His visit there placed particular emphasis on the invitation of the organizing committee of the Lake Mohonk Peace Conference for Him to address this international gathering. He had also been generous in His encouragement of the Central Organization for a Durable Peace at The Hague. He was, however, entirely candid in the counsel He provided. Letters which the Executive Committee of The Hague organization had written to Him during the course of the war provided the opportunity for a response that drew the organizers' attention to Bahá'u'lláh's enunciation of spiritual truths which alone can provide a foundation for the realization of their aims:

> O ye esteemed ones who are pioneers among the well-wishers of the world of humanity!… At present Universal Peace is a matter of great importance, but unity of conscience is essential, so that the foundation of this matter may become secure, its establishment firm and its edifice strong…. Today nothing but the power of the Word of God which encompasses the realities of things can bring the thoughts, the minds, the hearts and the spirits under the shade of one Tree. He is the potent in all things, the vivifier of souls, the preserver and the controller of the world of mankind.[132]

Beyond this, the list of influential persons with whom the Master spent patient hours in both North America and Europe—particularly individuals struggling to promote the goal of world peace and humanitarianism—reflects His awareness of the responsibility the Cause has to humanity at large. As the extraordinary response evoked by His passing testifies, He pursued this course to the end of His life.

Shoghi Effendi took up this legacy almost immediately upon beginning his ministry. As early as 1925, he encouraged the interest of an American believer, Jean Stannard, to establish an "International Bahá'í Bureau", directing her to Geneva, seat of the League of Nations. While the Bureau exercised no administrative authority, it acted, in the Guardian's words, "as intermediary between Haifa and other Bahá'í centers" and served as an information "distributing center" in the heart of Europe, its role being formally recognized when the League's publishing house solicited and published an account of the Bureau's activities.[133]

As has so often been the case in the history of the Cause, an unexpected crisis served to greatly advance Bahá'í involvement with the larger society at the international level. In 1928, Shoghi Effendi encouraged the Spiritual Assembly of Baghdad to appeal to the League's Permanent Mandates Commission against the seizure, by Shí'ih opponents, of Bahá'u'lláh's House in that city. Recognizing the wrong that had been done, the Council of the League unanimously called on the British mandate authority, in March 1929, to press the Iraqi government "with a view to the immediate redress of the injustice suffered by the Petitioners". Repeated evasions by the Iraqi government, including the violation of a solemn pledge on the part of the monarch himself, resulted in the case dragging on for years through successive sessions of the Mandates Commission, leaving the House in the hands of those who had seized it, a situation that remains to this day uncorrected.[134] Undeterred by this failure, Shoghi Effendi focused the attention of the Bahá'í community on the historic benefit that the campaign had won for the Cause. As had earlier been the case with the Sunni Muslim court's rejection of the appeal of an Egyptian Bahá'í community regarding marriage, the Guardian pointed out:

> Suffice it to say that, despite these interminable delays, protests and evasions … the publicity achieved for the Faith by this memorable litigation, and the defence of its cause—the cause of truth and justice—by the world's highest tribunal, have been such as to excite the wonder of its friends and to fill with consternation its enemies.[135]

The birth of the United Nations opened to the Faith a far broader and more effective forum for its efforts toward exerting a spiritual influence on the life of society. As early as 1947, a special "Palestine Committee" of the United Nations solicited the views of the Guardian on the future of that mandated territory. His response to the inquiry provided an opportunity for him to forward an authoritative exposition of the history and teachings of the Cause itself. That same year, with Shoghi Effendi's encouragement, the National Spiritual Assembly of the United States and Canada submitted to the international organization a document entitled "A Bahá'í Declaration on Human Obligations and Rights", which was to inspire the work of Bahá'í writers and spokespersons over the decades that followed.[136] A year later the eight National Spiritual Assemblies then in existence secured from the responsible United Nations body accreditation for "The Bahá'í International Community" as an international non-governmental organization.

It was not only the Faith's slowly emerging relationship with the new international order that elicited support of this kind from the Guardian. The pages of *God Passes By* and Amatu'l-Bahá's memoirs of the Guardian are filled with references to responses that influential individuals and organizations made to initiatives taken by Shoghi Effendi and to the events around the world in which Bahá'í representatives were invited to participate. In the perspective of history, one is struck by the vast disparity between many of these relatively inconsequential occasions and the attention given them by a figure whose work was not only of enormous importance to humanity's future, but who understood fully the relative significance of events unfolding around him. What the Bahá'í community has been given in this careful record is a guide to the way that it must take up the growing opportunities born out of modest beginnings.

From the moment of its accreditation, the Bahá'í International Community began to play an energetic role in United Nations' affairs. An activity that won it much appreciation was a programme carried out, through the expanding network of Bahá'í Assemblies, to provide the public with information about the United Nations itself, and which gave generous support to struggling United Nations associations throughout the world. By 1970, the Community had secured consultative status with the United Nations Economic and Social Council (ECOSOC). This was followed in 1974 by the granting of formal association with the United Nations Environmental Programme (UNEP) and in 1976 by the acquisition of consultative status with the United Nations Children's Fund

(UNICEF). The influence and expertise developed during these years showed their capacity, in 1955 and 1962, when the Community was successful in securing United Nations' intervention on behalf of the believers suffering persecution in Iran and Morocco, respectively.

In 1980, the patient external affairs activities of the National Spiritual Assemblies and the Community's United Nations Office were suddenly propelled into a new stage of their development. The catalyst was the attempt by the <u>Sh</u>í'ih clergy of Iran to exterminate the Cause in the land of its birth. The consequences were as little anticipated by the Faith's persecutors as they were by its defenders.

Throughout the long decades in which the believers in the cradle of the Faith suffered intermittent persecution for their beliefs, the mullás, who instigated and led these attacks, acted in concert with the country's succession of monarchs. The latter, ostensibly absolute in their authority, were in fact constrained by political calculations that rendered them vulnerable to outside pressures, particularly from Western governments. So it was that the outrage voiced by Russian, British and other diplomatic missions had compelled Náṣiri'd-Dín <u>Sh</u>áh, against his will, to bring to an end the orgy of violence that took so many believers' lives in the early 1850s and threatened that of Bahá'u'lláh Himself. During the twentieth century, his Qájár successors had been similarly concerned to placate the opinion of foreign governments. The pattern was repeated in 1955 when the second of the Pahlaví shahs, who had been induced by the mullás to approve a wave of anti-Bahá'í violence, was forced by United Nations' protest and by objections on the part of the American government to abruptly halt the campaign—both interventions harbingers of things to come.

Such checks on the clergy's behaviour seemed to have been swept away by the Islamic revolution of 1979. Suddenly, the mullás were themselves in power, appointing their own nominees to the highest positions in the new republic, and eventually taking over these posts directly. "Revolutionary

courts" were set up, answering only to the senior clergy. An army of "revolutionary guards", far more effective than the shah's secret police, and quite
as brutal, took over control of every aspect of public life.

While the attention of the new ruling caste was focused chiefly on
what it believed were threats from foreign governments, influential elements within it saw an opportunity at last to destroy the Iranian Bahá'í
community.[137] The harrowing details of the campaign that followed
need no review here. Their significance lies, rather, in the response
made to these attacks by thousands of individual Bahá'ís—men,
women and children—throughout the country. Their refusal to compromise their faith, even at the cost of their lives, inspired in their
fellow believers throughout the world a heightened dedication to the
Cause for which these sacrifices were being made. It was not, however,
only the members of the Faith who were affected by these events. Decades earlier, in 1889, a distinguished Western commentator on the
heroism of the dawn-breakers of the Faith had prophetically written of
the sufferings of the early believers:

> It is the lives and deaths of these, their hope which knows no despair,
> their love which knows no cooling, their steadfastness which knows
> no wavering, which stamp this wonderful movement with a character
> entirely its own…. It is not a small or easy thing to endure what these
> have endured, and surely what they deemed worth life itself is worth
> trying to understand. I say nothing of the mighty influence which, as
> I believe, the Bábí [sic] faith will exert in the future, nor of the new
> life it may perchance breathe into a dead people; for, whether it suc-
> ceed or fail, the splendid heroism of the Bábí martyrs is a thing eternal
> and indestructible…. But what I cannot hope to have conveyed to
> you is the terrible earnestness of these men, and the indescribable in-
> fluence which this earnestness, combined with other qualities, exerts
> on any one who has actually been brought in contact with them.[138]

These words prefigured the rise of a similar sentiment among non-Bahá'í
observers during the Islamic revolutionary years; and this was to become
one of the most powerful forces propelling the emergence of the Cause
from obscurity. Captured in those early words, too, was the fundamentally

spiritual nature of what has always been at stake in the cradle of the Faith. Beyond a revulsion at the senseless brutality of the persecution, a growing body of foreign opinion has been profoundly moved by the response of the Iranian Bahá'ís.

The twentieth century has, alas, been overwhelmed by the suffering of countless victims of oppression. What made the Bahá'í situation unique was the attitude adopted by those who endured the suffering. The Iranian believers refused to accept the all too familiar role of victims. Like the Founders of the Faith before them, they took moral charge of the great issue between them and their adversaries. It was they, not revolutionary courts or revolutionary guards, who quickly set the terms of the encounter, and this extraordinary achievement affected not only the hearts but the minds of those who observed the situation from outside the Bahá'í Faith. The persecuted community neither attacked its oppressors, nor sought political advantage from the crisis. Nor did its Bahá'í defenders in other lands call for the dismantling of the Iranian constitution, much less for revenge. All demanded only justice —the recognition of the rights guaranteed by the Universal Declaration of Human Rights, endorsed by the community of nations, ratified by the Iranian government, and many of them embodied even in clauses of the Islamic constitution.

The crisis roused the Bahá'í world to extraordinary feats of achievement. National Spiritual Assemblies who had little or no experience in developing a working relationship with officials of their countries' governments were called on to solicit government support for resolutions at various levels of the international human rights system, and did so with outstanding success. Year after year, for twenty uninterrupted years, the case of the Iranian Bahá'ís proceeded through the international human rights system, gathering support in successive resolutions, ensuring attention to Bahá'í grievances in the missions of rapporteurs appointed by the United Nations Human Rights Commission and consolidating these gains through decisions of the Third Committee of the United Nations General Assembly. Every attempt by the Iranian regime to escape international condemnation of its treatment of its Bahá'í citizens failed to shake the support the Bahá'í issue attracted from a persistent majority of

sympathetic nations represented on the Commission. The achievement
was all the more remarkable in the context of the Commission's constantly
changing membership and a demanding agenda that included human
rights abuses in other countries that affected millions of victims.

At the same time as direct pressure was being exerted on the Iranian
government, the case was attracting unprecedented publicity around
the world in newspapers, magazines and the broadcast media. Newspapers such as *The New York Times*, *Le Monde* and *Frankfurter Allgemeine
Zeitung*, enjoying international readership, gave wide coverage to the
persecution, and television networks in Australia, Canada, the United
States and a number of European countries produced in-depth, maga-
zine-format presentations. The abuses were denounced in often strong
editorial comment. Apart from the support thus lent to the efforts to
secure effective intervention at the Human Rights Commission, such
publicity had the effect of introducing, usually for the first time and to
an audience of tens of millions of people, accurate and appreciative information about Bahá'í teachings and belief. Both the publicity and the
campaign being carried on through the United Nations' system provided influential officials around the world with a sustained
opportunity to judge for themselves both the teachings of the Cause
and the character of the Bahá'í community.

A problem arising out of the persecution was that faced by several thousand Iranian Bahá'ís who found themselves either stranded without valid
passports in countries where they were serving as pioneers, or forced to flee
from Iran because they or their families had been singled out as targets of
the pogrom. In 1983, an International Bahá'í Refugee Office was established in Canada,[139] where the government had been particularly responsive
to the representations made by the National Spiritual Assembly of that
country. Over the next few years, with the assistance of the United Nations
High Commission for Refugees, a series of other countries likewise opened
their doors to more than ten thousand Iranian Bahá'ís, many of whom
filled pioneer goals in their new places of residence.

✳

Not only the Bahá'í community but the United Nations' human rights system itself benefited from this long struggle. Initially, after the Islamic revolution, the community of believers in Iran had faced a threat to its very survival. In time, the United Nations Human Rights Commission, however slow and relatively cumbersome its operations may appear to some outside observers, succeeded in compelling the Iranian regime to bring the worst of the persecution to a halt. In this way, the "case of Iran's Bahá'ís" marked a significant victory for the Commission and the Bahá'í Faith alike. It served as a startling demonstration of the power of the community of nations, acting through the machinery created for the purpose, to bring under control patterns of oppression that had darkened the pages of recorded history throughout the ages.

This circumstance highlights the relevance of the Faith's activities to the life of the larger society in which these efforts are taking place. Together with world peace, the need for the international community to take effective steps to realize the ideals in the Universal Declaration of Human Rights and its related covenants is an urgent challenge facing humanity at the present moment in its history. There are relatively few places in the world where minority populations, because of religious, ethnic or national prejudices, are not still denied basic human needs of some kind. No body of people on the planet understands better this issue than does the Bahá'í community. It has endured—continues to endure in some lands—mistreatment for which there is no conceivable justification, whether legal or moral; it has given its martyrs and shed its tears, while remaining faithful to its conviction that hatred and retaliation are corrosive to the soul; and it has learned, as few communities have done, how to use the United Nations' human rights system in the manner intended by that system's creators, without having recourse to involvement in political partisanship of any kind, much less violence. Drawing on this experience, it is today embarked on a programme to encourage governments in a score of countries to institute public education programmes on the subject of human rights, providing whatever practical assistance of its own is possible.[140] Throughout the world, it is particularly active in promoting the rights of women and children. Most important of all, it provides a living example of brotherhood, from which countless people outside its embrace derive courage and hope.

As the Iranian crisis was unfolding, an initiative taken by the Universal House of Justice suddenly moved the external affairs work of the Bahá'í community to an entirely new level. In 1985, the statement *The Promise of World Peace*, addressed to the generality of humankind, was released through National Spiritual Assemblies. In it, the House of Justice asserted, in unprovocative but uncompromising terms, Bahá'í confidence in the advent of international peace as the next stage in the evolution of society. Set out, as well, were elements of the form that this long-awaited development must take, many of which went far beyond the political terms in which the subject is commonly discussed. It concluded:

> The experience of the Bahá'í community may be seen as an example of this enlarging unity [of humankind].... If the Bahá'í experience can contribute in whatever measure to reinforcing hope in the unity of the human race, we are happy to offer it as a model for study.

While the immediate purpose of the release was to provide Bahá'í institutions and individual believers with a coherent line of discussion for their interactions with government authorities, organizations of civil society, the media and influential personalities, a collateral effect was to set in motion an intensive and ongoing education of the Bahá'í community itself in several important Bahá'í teachings. The influence of the ideas and perspectives in the document was soon making itself widely felt in conventions, publications, summer and winter schools, and the general discourse of believers everywhere.

In many respects, *The Promise of World Peace* may be said to have set the agenda for Bahá'í interaction with the United Nations and its attendant organizations in the years since 1985. Building on the reputation it had already won, the Bahá'í International Community became, in only a few short years, one of the most influential of the non-governmental organizations. Because it is, and is seen to be, entirely non-partisan, it has increasingly been trusted as a mediating voice in complex, and often stressful, discussions in international circles on major issues of social progress. This reputation has been strengthened by appreciation of the fact that the Community refrains, on principle, from taking advantage of such trust to press partisan agendas of its own. By 1968, a Bahá'í representative had been elected to membership on the Executive Committee of Non-Governmental Organizations affiliated with the Office of Public Information, subsequently holding the positions of chairman and vice-chairman. From this point on, representatives of the Community found themselves increasingly asked to function as convenors or chairpersons of a wide range of bodies: committees, task forces, working groups and advisory boards. During the past four years, the Community has served as executive secretary of the Conference of Non-Governmental Organizations, the central coordinating body of non-governmental groups affiliated with the United Nations.

The structure of the Bahá'í International Community reflects the principles guiding its work. It has escaped labelling as merely another special interest lobby group. While making full use of the expertise and executive resources of its United Nations Office and Office of Public Information, the Community has come to be recognized by its fellow non-governmental organizations as essentially an "association" of democratically elected national "councils", representative of a cross-section of humankind. Bahá'í delegations to international events commonly include members appointed by various National Spiritual Assemblies who are experienced in the subject matters under discussion and who can provide regional perspectives.

This feature of the Faith's involvement in the life of society—in which motivating principle and operating method represent two dimensions of a unified approach to issues—demonstrated its power at the series of world summits and related conferences organized by the United Nations held between 1990 and 1996. In that period of nearly six years, the political leaders of the world came together repeatedly under the aegis of the Secretary-General of the United Nations to discuss the major challenges facing humankind as the twentieth century drew to a close. No Bahá'í can review the themes of these historic gatherings without being struck by how closely the agenda mirrored major teachings of Bahá'u'lláh. It seemed befitting that the centenary of His ascension should occur at the midway point in the process, endowing the meetings, for Bahá'ís, with spiritual meaning beyond merely their stated goals.

Among those gatherings, the World Conference on Education for All in Thailand (1990), the World Summit for Children in New York (1990), the United Nations Conference on the Environment in Rio de Janeiro (1992), an anguished and chaotic World Conference on Human Rights in Vienna (1993), the International Conference on Population in Cairo (1994), the World Summit for Social Development in Copenhagen (1995), and the particularly vibrant Fourth World Conference on Women in Beijing (1995),[141] stand out as highlights of this process of global discourse on the problems afflicting the world's peoples. At the concurrent non-governmental conferences, Bahá'í delegations, made up of members from a wide range of countries, had the opportunity to place issues in a spiritual as well as social perspective. Evidence of the trust the Community enjoys among hundreds of its fellow non-governmental organizations was the fact that Bahá'í delegations were repeatedly selected by their peers for inclusion among the handful of member groups to be accorded the much prized opportunity to address the conferences from the podium, rather than merely distributing printed copies of presentations.

During the century's concluding years, many National Spiritual Assemblies won impressive victories of their own in the field of external affairs. Two outstanding examples suggest the character and importance of these advances. The first was achieved by the National Spiritual Assembly of Germany, where the nature of Bahá'í elected bodies had been challenged by local authorities as being technically incompatible with the requirements of German civil law. In upholding the appeal of the Local Spiritual Assembly of the Bahá'ís of Tübingen against this ruling,

Germany's constitutional High Court concluded that the Bahá'í Administrative Order is an integral feature of the Faith and as such is inseparable from Bahá'í belief. The High Court justified its taking jurisdiction in the case by adducing evidence that the Bahá'í Faith itself is a religion, a judgement with far-reaching implications in a society where church opponents have long sought to misrepresent the Cause as a "cult" or "sect". The definitive language of the judgement merits repetition:

> ...the character of the Bahá'í Faith as a religion and of the Bahá'í Community as a religious community is evident, in actual every day life, in cultural tradition, and in the understanding of the general public as well as of the science of comparative religion.[142]

It was left to the Brazilian Bahá'í community to win a victory in the field of external affairs that is so far unique in Bahá'í history. On 28 May 1992, its country's highest legislative body, the Chamber of Deputies, held a special session to pay tribute to Bahá'u'lláh on the centenary of His ascension. The Speaker read a message from the Universal House of Justice and representatives of all of the parties rose, one by one, to acknowledge the contribution to human betterment of the Faith and its Founder. A moving address by one prominent deputy described the Bahá'í teachings as "the most colossal religious work ever written by the pen of a single Man".[143]

Such appreciations of the nature of the Cause and of the work it is trying to accomplish—coming as they did from the highest judicial and legislative levels, respectively, of two of the world's major nations—were victories of the spirit as important in their way as those won in the teaching field. They help to open those doors through which Bahá'u'lláh's healing influence begins to touch the life of society itself.

XI

THE IMAGE USED BY 'ABDU'L-BAHÁ to capture for His hearers the coming transformation of society was that of light. Unity, He declared, is the power that illuminates and advances all forms of human endeavour. The age that was opening would come in the future to be regarded as "the century of light", because in it universal recognition of the oneness of humankind would be achieved. With this foundation in place, the process of building a global society embodying principles of justice will begin.

The vision was enunciated by the Master in several Tablets and addresses. Its fullest expression occurs in a Tablet addressed by 'Abdu'l-Bahá to Jane Elizabeth Whyte, wife of the former Moderator of the Free Church of Scotland. Mrs. Whyte was an ardent sympathizer of the Bahá'í teachings, had visited the Master in 'Akká and would later make arrangements for the particularly warm reception that met Him in Edinburgh. Using the familiar metaphor of "candles", 'Abdu'l-Bahá wrote to Mrs. Whyte:

> O honored lady!… Behold how its [unity's] light is now dawning upon the world's darkened horizon. The first candle is unity in the political realm, the early glimmerings of which can now be discerned. The second candle is unity of thought in world undertakings, the

consummation of which will erelong be witnessed. The third candle is
unity in freedom which will surely come to pass. The fourth candle is
unity in religion which is the corner-stone of the foundation itself,
and which, by the power of God, will be revealed in all its splendor.
The fifth candle is the unity of nations—a unity which in this century will be securely established, causing all the peoples of the world
to regard themselves as citizens of one common fatherland. The sixth
candle is unity of races, making of all that dwell on earth peoples and
kindreds of one race. The seventh candle is unity of language, i.e., the
choice of a universal tongue in which all peoples will be instructed
and converse. Each and every one of these will inevitably come to
pass, inasmuch as the power of the Kingdom of God will aid and assist in their realization.[144]

While it will be decades—or perhaps a great deal longer—before the
vision contained in this remarkable document is fully realized, the essential features of what it promised are now established facts throughout the
world. In several of the great changes envisioned—unity of race and
unity of religion—the intent of the Master's words is clear and the processes involved are far advanced, however great may be the resistance in
some quarters. To a large extent this is also true of unity of language. The
need for it is now recognized on all sides, as reflected in the circumstances that have compelled the United Nations and much of the
non-governmental community to adopt several "official languages". Until a decision is taken by international agreement, the effect of such
developments as the Internet, the management of air traffic, the development of technological vocabularies of various kinds, and universal
education itself, has been to make it possible, to some extent, for English
to fill the gap.

"Unity of thought in world undertakings", a concept for which the
most idealistic aspirations at the opening of the twentieth century lacked
even reference points, is also in large measure everywhere apparent in vast
programmes of social and economic development, humanitarian aid and
concern for protection of the environment of the planet and its oceans.
As to "unity in the political realm", Shoghi Effendi has explained that the

reference is to unity which sovereign states achieve among themselves, a developing process the present stage of which is the establishment of the United Nations. The Master's promise of "unity of nations", on the other hand, looked forward to today's widespread acceptance among the peoples of the world of the fact that, however great the differences among them may be, they are the inhabitants of a single global homeland.

"Unity in freedom" has today, of course, become a universal aspiration of the Earth's inhabitants. Among the chief developments giving substance to it, the Master may well have had in mind the dramatic extinction of colonialism and the consequent rise of self-determination as a dominant feature of national identity at century's end.

Whatever threats still hang over humanity's future, the world has been transformed by the events of the twentieth century. That the features of the process should also have been described by the Voice that predicted it with such confidence ought to command earnest reflection on the part of serious minds everywhere.

The changes wrought in humanity's social and moral life received powerful endorsement at a series of international gatherings called under the United Nations' authority to mark the approaching end of one "millennium" and the beginning of a new one. On 22-26 May 2000, representatives of over one thousand non-governmental organizations assembled in New York at the invitation of Kofi Annan, the United Nations Secretary-General. In the statement that emerged from this meeting, spokespersons of civil society committed their organizations to the ideal that: "…we are one human family, in all our diversity, living on one common homeland and sharing a just, sustainable and peaceful world, guided by universal principles of democracy…."[145]

Shortly afterwards, from 28-31 August 2000, a second gathering brought together leaders of most of the world's religious communities, likewise assembled at the United Nations Headquarters. The Bahá'í International Community was represented by its Secretary-General, who addressed one of the plenary sessions. No observer could fail to be struck by the call of the world's religious leaders, formally, for their communities "to respect the right to freedom of religion, to seek reconciliation, and to engage in mutual forgiveness and healing…."[146]

These two preliminary events prepared the way for what had been designated as the Millennium Summit itself, meeting at the United Nations Headquarters from 6-8 September 2000. Bringing together 149 heads of state and government, the consultation sought to give hope and assurance to the populations of the nations represented. The Summit took the welcome step of inviting a spokesman for the Forum of non-governmental organizations to share the concerns that had been identified at that preparatory gathering. It seemed to Bahá'ís as significant as it was gratifying that the individual accorded this high honour was the Bahá'í International Community's Principal Representative to the United Nations, in his capacity as Co-Chairman of the Forum. Nothing so dramatically illustrates the difference between the world of 1900 and that of 2000 than the text of the Summit Resolution, signed by all the participants, and referred by them to the United Nations General Assembly:

> We solemnly reaffirm, on this historic occasion, that the United Nations is the indispensable common house of the entire human family, through which we will seek to realize our universal aspirations for peace, cooperation and development. We therefore pledge our unstinting support for these common objectives, and our determination to achieve them.[147]

In concluding this sequence of historic meetings, Mr. Annan addressed himself to the assembled world leaders in surprisingly candid terms—terms that, for many Bahá'ís, carried echoes of Bahá'u'lláh's stern admonition to the now vanished kings and emperors who had been these leaders' predecessors: "It lies in *your* power, and therefore it is your responsibility, to reach the goals that you have defined. Only *you* can determine whether the United Nations rises to the challenge."[148]

*

Despite the historic importance of the meetings and the fact that the greater portion of humanity's political, civil and religious leadership took part, the Millennium Summit made little impression on the public mind in most countries. Generous media attention was given to certain of the events, but few readers or listeners could fail to note the expression of scepticism that characterized editorial treatment of the subject or the air of doubt—even of cynicism—that crept into many of the news stories themselves. This sharp disjunction between an event that could legitimately claim to mark a major turning-point in human history, on the one hand, and the lack of enthusiasm or even interest it aroused among populations who were its supposed beneficiaries, on the other, was perhaps the most striking feature of the millennium observations. It exposed the depth of the crisis the world is experiencing at century's end, in which the processes of both integration and disintegration that had gathered momentum during the past hundred years seem to accelerate with each passing day.

Those who long to believe the visionary statements of world leaders struggle at the same time in the grip of two phenomena that undermine such confidence. The first has already been considered at some length in these pages. The collapse of society's moral foundations has left the greater part of humankind floundering without reference points in a world that grows daily more threatening and unpredictable. To suggest that the process has nearly reached its end would be merely to raise false hopes. One may appreciate that intense political efforts are being made, that impressive scientific advances continue or that economic conditions improve for a portion of humankind—all without seeing in such developments anything resembling hope of a secure life for oneself, or more importantly, for one's children. The sense of disillusionment which, as Shoghi Effendi warned, the spread of political corruption would create in the minds of the mass of humankind is now widespread. Outbreaks of lawlessness have become pandemic in both urban and rural life in many lands. The failure of social controls, the effort to justify the most extreme forms of aberrant behaviour as primarily civil rights issues, and an almost universal celebration in the arts and media of degeneracy and violence—

these and similar manifestations of a condition approaching moral anarchy suggest a future that paralyzes the imagination. Against the
background of this desolate landscape the intellectual vogue of the age,
seeking to make a virtue out of grim necessity, has adopted for itself the
appellation and mission of "deconstructionism".

The second of the two developments undermining faith in the future was the focus of some of the Millennium Summit's most anguished
debates. The information revolution set off in the closing decade of the
century by the invention of the World Wide Web transformed irreversibly much of human activity. The process of "globalization" that had
been following a long rising curve over a period of several centuries was
galvanized by new powers beyond the imaginations of most people.
Economic forces, breaking free of traditional restraints, brought into
being during the closing decade of the century a new global order in
the designing, generation and distribution of wealth. Knowledge itself
became a significantly more valuable commodity than even financial
capital and material resources. In a breathtakingly short space of time,
national borders, already under assault, became permeable, with the result that vast sums now pass instantly through them at the command of
a computer signal. Complex production operations are so reconfigured
as to integrate and maximize the economies available from the contributions of a range of specializing participants, without regard to their
national locations. If one were to lower one's horizon to purely material
considerations, the earth has already taken on something of the character of "one country" and the inhabitants of various lands the status of
its consumer "citizens".

Nor is the transformation merely economic. Increasingly, globalization assumes political, social and cultural dimensions. It has become clear
that the powers of the institution of the nation-state, once the arbiter and
protector of humanity's fortunes, have been drastically eroded. While
national governments continue to play a crucial role, they must now
make room for such rising centres of power as multinational corporations, United Nations agencies, non-governmental organizations of every
kind, and huge media conglomerates, the cooperation of all of which is
vital to the success of most programmes aimed at achieving significant

economic or social ends. Just as the migration of money or corporations encounters little hindrance from national borders, neither can the latter any longer exercise effective control over the dissemination of knowledge. Internet communication, which has the ability to transmit in seconds the entire contents of libraries that took centuries of study to amass, vastly enriches the intellectual life of anyone able to use it, as well as providing sophisticated training in a broad range of professional fields. The system, so prophetically foreseen sixty years ago by Shoghi Effendi, builds a sense of shared community among its users that is impatient of either geographic or cultural distances.

The benefits to many millions of persons are obvious and impressive. Cost effectiveness resulting from the coordination of formerly competing operations tends to bring goods and services within the reach of populations who could not previously have hoped to enjoy them. Enormous increases in the funds available for research and development expand the variety and quality of such benefits. Something of a levelling effect in the distribution of employment opportunities can be seen in the ease with which business operations can shift their base from one part of the world to another. The abandonment of barriers to transnational trade reduces still further the cost of goods to consumers. It is not difficult to appreciate, from a Bahá'í perspective, the potentiality of such transformations for laying the foundations of the global society envisioned in Bahá'u'lláh's Writings.

Far from inspiring optimism about the future, however, globalization is seen by large and growing numbers of people around the world as the principal threat to that future. The violence of the riots set off by the meetings of the World Trade Organization, the World Bank and the International Monetary Fund during the last two years testifies to the depth of the fear and resentment that the rise of globalization has provoked. Media coverage of these unexpected outbursts focused public attention on protests against gross disparities in the distribution of benefits and opportunities, which globalization is seen as only increasing, and on warnings that, if effective controls are not speedily imposed, the consequences will be catastrophic in social and political, as well as in economic and environmental, terms.

Such concerns appear well-founded. Economic statistics alone reveal
a picture of current global conditions that is profoundly disturbing. The
ever-widening gulf between the one fifth of the world's population living
in the highest income countries and the one fifth living in the lowest income countries tells a grim story. According to the 1999 Human
Development Report published by the United Nations Development Programme, this gap represented, in 1990, a ratio of sixty to one. That is to
say, one segment of humankind was enjoying access to sixty percent of
the world's wealth, while another, equally large, population struggled
merely to survive on barely one percent of that wealth. By 1997, in the
wake of globalization's rapid advance, the gulf had widened in only seven
years to a ratio of seventy-four to one. Even this appalling fact does not
take into account the steady impoverishment of the majority of the remaining billions of human beings trapped in the relentlessly narrowing
isthmus between these two extremes. Far from being brought under control, the crisis is clearly accelerating. The implications for humanity's
future, in terms of privation and despair engulfing more than two thirds
of the Earth's population, helped to account for the apathy that met the
Millennium Summit's celebration of achievements that were, by all
reasonable criteria, truly historic.

Globalization itself is an intrinsic feature of the evolution of human
society. It has brought into existence a socio-economic culture that, at the
practical level, constitutes the world in which the aspirations of the human race will be pursued in the century now opening. No objective
observer, if he is fair-minded in his judgement, will deny that both of the
two contradictory reactions it is arousing are, in large measure, well justified. The unification of human society, forged by the fires of the
twentieth century, is a reality that with every passing day opens breath-
taking new possibilities. A reality also being forced on serious minds
everywhere, is the claim of justice to be the one means capable of har-
nessing these great potentialities to the advancement of civilization. It no
longer requires the gift of prophecy to realize that the fate of humanity in
the century now opening will be determined by the relationship established between these two fundamental forces of the historical process, the
inseparable principles of unity and justice.

In the perspective of Bahá'u'lláh's teachings, the greatest danger of both the moral crisis and the inequities associated with globalization in its current form is an entrenched philosophical attitude that seeks to justify and excuse these failures. The overthrow of the twentieth century's totalitarian systems has not meant the end of ideology. On the contrary. There has not been a society in the history of the world, no matter how pragmatic, experimentalist and multi-form it may have been, that did not derive its thrust from some foundational interpretation of reality. Such a system of thought reigns today virtually unchallenged across the planet, under the nominal designation "Western civilization". Philosophically and politically, it presents itself as a kind of liberal relativism; economically and socially, as capitalism—two value systems that have now so adjusted to each other and become so mutually reinforcing as to constitute virtually a single, comprehensive world-view.

Appreciation of the benefits—in terms of the personal freedom, social prosperity and scientific progress enjoyed by a significant minority of the Earth's people—cannot withhold a thinking person from recognizing that the system is morally and intellectually bankrupt. It has contributed its best to the advancement of civilization, as did all its predecessors, and, like them, is impotent to deal with the needs of a world never imagined by the eighteenth century prophets who conceived most of its component elements. Shoghi Effendi did not limit his attention to divine right monarchies, established churches or totalitarian ideologies when he posed the searching question: "Why should these, in a world subject to the immutable law of change and decay, be exempt from the deterioration that must needs overtake every human institution?"[149]

Bahá'u'lláh urges those who believe in Him to "see with thine own eyes and not through the eyes of others", to "know of thine own knowledge and not through the knowledge of thy neighbour". Tragically, what Bahá'ís see in present-day society is unbridled exploitation of the masses of humanity by greed that excuses itself as the operation of "impersonal market forces". What meets their eyes everywhere is the destruction of moral foundations vital to humanity's future, through gross self-indulgence masquerading as "freedom of speech". What they find themselves struggling against daily is the pressure of a dogmatic materialism, claiming to be the voice of "science", that seeks systematically to exclude from intellectual life all impulses arising from the spiritual level of human consciousness.

And for a Bahá'í the ultimate issues *are* spiritual. The Cause is not a political party nor an ideology, much less an engine for political agitation against this or that social wrong. The process of transformation it has set in motion advances by inducing a fundamental change of consciousness, and the challenge it poses to everyone who would serve it is to free oneself from attachment to inherited assumptions and preferences that are irreconcilable with the Will of God for humanity's coming of age. Paradoxically, even the distress caused by prevailing conditions that violate one's conscience aids in this process of spiritual liberation. In the final analysis, such disillusionment drives a Bahá'í to confront a truth emphasized over and over again in the Writings of the Faith:

> He hath chosen out of the whole world the hearts of His servants, and made them each a seat for the revelation of His glory. Wherefore, sanctify them from every defilement, that the things for which they were created may be engraven upon them.[150]

XII

THE OPENING STATEMENT OF THE GOSPEL attributed to Jesus' disciple, John—"In the beginning was the Word…"—has fascinated readers for two thousand years. The passage goes on to assert with breath-taking simplicity and directness a spiritual truth that has been central to all revealed religions, vindicated time and again in a succession of civilizations down the ages: "He was in the world, and the world was made by Him". The promised Manifestation of God appears; a community of believers forms around this focal centre of spiritual life and authority; a new system of values begins to reorder both consciousness and behaviour; the arts and sciences respond; a restructuring of laws and of the administration of social affairs takes place. Slowly, but irresistibly, a new civilization emerges, one that so fulfils the ideals and so engages the capacities of millions of human beings that it does indeed constitute a new world, a world far more real to those who "live, move, and have their being"[151] in it than the earthly foun-dations on which it rests. Throughout the centuries that follow, society continues to depend for its cohesion and self-confidence primarily on the spiritual impulse that gave it birth.

With the appearance of Bahá'u'lláh, the phenomenon has recurred —this time on a scale that embraces the totality of the earth's inhabit-ants. In the events of the twentieth century can be seen the first stages of the universal transformation of society set in motion by the Revelation of which Bahá'u'lláh wrote:

> I testify that no sooner had the First Word proceeded, through the potency of Thy will and purpose, out of His mouth ... than the whole creation was revolutionized, and all that are in the heavens and all that are on earth were stirred to the depths. Through that Word the realities of all created things were shaken, were divided, separated, scattered, combined and reunited, disclosing, in both the contingent world and the heavenly kingdom, entities of a new creation, and revealing, in the unseen realms, the signs and tokens of Thy unity and oneness.[152]

Shoghi Effendi describes this process of world unification as the "Major Plan" of God, whose operation will continue, gathering force and momentum, until the human race has been united in a global society that has banished war and taken charge of its collective destiny. What the struggles of the twentieth century achieved was the fundamental change of direction the Divine purpose required. The change is irreversible. There is no way back to an earlier state of affairs, however greatly some elements of society may, from time to time, be tempted to seek one.

The importance of the historic breakthrough that has thus occurred is in no way minimized by recognition that the process has barely begun. It must lead in time, as Shoghi Effendi has made clear, to the spiritualization of human consciousness and the emergence of the global civilization that will embody the Will of God. Merely to state the goal is to acknowledge the great distance that the human race has yet to traverse. It was against the most intense resistance at every level of society, among governed and governors alike, that the political, social and conceptual changes of the past hundred years were achieved. Ultimately, they were accomplished only at the cost of terrible suffering. It would be unrealistic to imagine that the challenges lying ahead may not exact an even greater toll of a human race that still seeks, by every means in its power, to avoid the spiritual implications of the experience it is undergoing. Shoghi Effendi's words on the consequences of this obduracy of heart and mind make sober reading:

Adversities unimaginably appalling, undreamed of crises and upheavals, war, famine, and pestilence, might well combine to engrave
in the soul of an unheeding generation those truths and principles
which it has disdained to recognize and follow.[153]

*

Barely a third of the twentieth century had elapsed when the
Guardian summoned the followers of Bahá'u'lláh to a far deeper understanding of the Cause itself than anything they had yet appreciated. The
Faith had reached the point, he said, when it was "ceasing to designate
itself a movement, a fellowship and the like", designations which, although perhaps appropriate at a time when the message was first being
introduced to the West, now "did grave injustice to its ever-unfolding
system". Rejecting as adequate even the term "religion" in its familiar
sense, he pointed out that the Faith was already:

> …visibly succeeding in demonstrating its claim and title to be re-
> garded as a World Religion, destined to attain, in the fullness of
> time, the status of a world-embracing Commonwealth, which would
> be at once the instrument and the guardian of the Most Great Peace
> announced by its Author.[154]

As the century advanced, the same creative Force that was awakening
the generality of humankind to its oneness was progressively releasing the
powers inherent in the Cause and opening a new role for it in human
affairs. Over the first two decades of the century, through the loving care
of the Master, the spiritual and administrative foundations necessary to
Bahá'u'lláh's purpose were established. On the base thus made available—
during the thirty-six years of his own ministry, and the subsequent six
years during which his Ten Year Crusade guided the community's efforts—Shoghi Effendi devoted himself to refining the administrative
instruments needed to carry forward the Divine Plan. With the successful establishment in 1963 of the Universal House of Justice, the Bahá'ís

of the world set out on the first stage of a mission of long duration: the spiritual empowerment of the whole body of humankind as the protagonists of their own advancement. By the time the century ended, this immense effort had brought into existence a community representative of the diversity of the entire human race, unified in its beliefs and allegiance, and committed to building a global society that will reflect on earth the spiritual and moral vision of its Founder.

This process was immeasurably strengthened in 1992 through the long-awaited publication of a fully-annotated translation into English of the Kitáb-i-Aqdas, a repository of Divine guidance for the age of humanity's collective maturity. A spreading circle of translations was soon providing followers of the Faith around the world with direct access to a Book which its Author has described as: "the Dayspring of Divine knowledge, if ye be of them that understand, and the Dawning-place of God's commandments, if ye be of those who comprehend."[155] Apart from the soul's recognition of the Manifestation of God, nothing awakens so great a sense of confidence and vitality in human consciousness—both individual and collective—as does the force of moral certitude. In the Kitáb-i-Aqdas, laws that are basic to both personal and community life have been reformulated in the context of a society that embraces the whole range of human diversity. New laws and concepts address the further needs of a human race that is entering on its collective coming of age. "O peoples of the earth!", is Bahá'u'lláh's appeal, "Cast away that which ye possess, and, on the wings of detachment, soar beyond all created things. Thus biddeth you the Lord of creation, the movement of Whose Pen hath revolutionized the soul of mankind."[156]

A feature of the past hundred years of Bahá'í development that should seize the attention of any observer is the Faith's success in overcoming the attacks made on it. As had been the case during the ministries of the Báb and Bahá'u'lláh, elements in society who either resented the rise of the new religion or feared the principles it teaches sought by every means in their power to suffocate it. Hardly a decade of the past century did not witness attempts of this kind—ranging from the bloody persecutions incited by Shí'ih clergy and the shameless falsehoods concocted and spread by their Christian counterparts, to systematic efforts at suppression by

various totalitarian regimes, and, finally, to violations of their commitment to Bahá'u'lláh on the part of the insincere, the ambitious or the
malevolent among its professed adherents. By every human standard, the
Cause should have succumbed to a barrage of opposition without parallel in recent history. Far from succumbing, it flourished. Its reputation
rose, its membership vastly increased, its influence spread beyond the
dreams of earlier generations of its followers. Persecution served to galva-
nize its supporters' efforts. Calumny drove believers to seek a more
mature understanding of its history and teachings. And, as both the
Master and the Guardian had promised, violation of the Covenant
washed out of its ranks persons whose behaviour and attitudes had damp-
ened the faith of others and inhibited progress. If the Cause could bring
no other testimony to the powers that sustain it, this succession of
triumphs alone should suffice.

Three years before his passing, Shoghi Effendi took advantage of the
acquisition of the last plot of land needed for the erection of the International Archives Building to describe for the Bahá'í world the nature and
significance of the building project on the slopes of Mount Carmel that
the Master had inaugurated and that he himself was pursuing:

> These Edifices will, in the shape of a far-flung arc, and following a
> harmonizing style of architecture, surround the resting-places of the
> Greatest Holy Leaf … of her Brother … and of their Mother…. The
> ultimate completion of this stupendous undertaking will mark the
> culmination of the development of a world-wide divinely-appointed
> Administrative Order whose beginnings may be traced as far back as
> the concluding years of the Heroic Age of the Faith.[157]

The current stage of this ambitious enterprise was brought to its successful conclusion in the final year of the century. An outpouring of
resources from believers throughout the world had responded to the
vision of Bahá'u'lláh for this sacred spot, announced in His Tablet of

Carmel: "Rejoice, for God hath in this day established upon thee His throne, hath made thee the dawning-place of His signs and the dayspring of the evidences of His Revelation." In the complex of majestic buildings spread out along the Arc and the flights of terraced gardens rising from the foot of the mountain to its summit, the Cause whose influence had steadily expanded throughout the world during the century of light emerged finally as a visible and compelling presence. In the crowds of visitors from every land thronging the stairs and pathways each day and the stream of distinguished guests who are welcomed to the World Centre's reception rooms, perceptive minds already sense the dawning fulfilment of the vision recorded twenty-three hundred years ago by the prophet Isaiah: "And it shall come to pass in the last days, *that* the mountain of the Lord's house shall be established in the top of the mountains, and shall be exalted above the hills; and all nations shall flow unto it."[158]

The Bahá'í Cause is distinguished above all else by its nature as an uncompromised organic whole. Embodying the principle of unity that lies at the heart of Bahá'u'lláh's Revelation, this nature is the sign of the presence of the indwelling Spirit that animates the Faith. Alone among the religions of history—and despite repeated efforts to break this unity—the Cause has successfully resisted the perennial blight of schism and faction. The success of the community's teaching work is assured by the fact that the instruments it uses were created by the Revelation itself, that it was the Faith's Founders who conceived the methods for the prosecution of its Divine Plan, and that it was They who guided, in every significant detail, the launching of the enterprise. During the twentieth century, through the efforts of 'Abdu'l-Bahá and the Guardian, Mount Carmel itself has become an expression of this oneness of the Faith's being. In contrast to the circumstances of other world religions, the spiritual and administrative centres of the Cause are inseparably bound together in this same spot on earth, its guiding institutions centred on the Shrine of its martyred Prophet. For many visitors, even the harmony that has been achieved in the variegated flowers, trees and shrubs of the surrounding gardens seems to proclaim the ideal of unity in diversity that they find attractive in the Faith's teachings.

Nothing so dramatically marked the conclusion of one hundred years of achievement as an event that also plunged believers the world over into deep sorrow. On 19 January 2000, a message from the Universal House of Justice announced:

> In the early hours of this morning, the soul of Amatu'l-Bahá Rúḥíyyih Khánum, beloved consort of Shoghi Effendi and the Bahá'í world's last remaining link with the family of 'Abdu'l-Bahá, was released from the limitations of this earthly existence.... Her twenty years of intimate association with Shoghi Effendi evoked from his pen such accolades as "my helpmate', 'my shield', 'my tireless collaborator in the arduous tasks I shoulder'....

As the initial shock of grief began to lift, appreciation of yet another of the inexhaustible bounties of Bahá'u'lláh gradually took its place. To a figure whose long lifetime had spanned most of the century—and whose indomitable spirit had sustained Bahá'í struggles and sacrifices throughout its latter half—it had been given to live and celebrate the magnificent victories to which she had so magnificently contributed.

In calling on those who have recognized Him to share the message of the Day of God with others, Bahá'u'lláh turns again to the language of creation itself: "Every body calleth aloud for a soul. Heavenly souls must needs quicken, with the breath of the Word of God, the dead bodies with a fresh spirit."[159] The principle is as true of the collective life of humankind, 'Abdu'l-Bahá points out, as it is of the lives of its individual members: "Material civilization is like the body. No matter how infinitely graceful, elegant and beautiful it may be, it is dead. Divine civilization is like the spirit, and the body gets its life from the spirit...."[160]

In this compelling analogy is summed up the relationship between the two historical developments that the Will of God propelled forward along converging tracks during the century of light. Only a person blind to the intellectual and social capacities latent in the human race, and insensitive to humanity's desperate needs, could fail to take deep satisfaction from the advances that society has made during the past hundred years, and particularly from the processes knitting together the earth's peoples and nations. How much more are such achievements cherished by Bahá'ís, who see in them the very Purpose of God. But this Body of humanity's material civilization calls aloud, yearns more desperately with each passing day, for its Soul. As with every great civilization in history, until it is so animated, and its spiritual faculties awakened, it will find neither peace, nor justice, nor a unity that rises above the level of negotiation and compromise. Addressing the "elected representatives of the people in every land", Bahá'u'lláh wrote:

> That which the Lord hath ordained as the sovereign remedy and mightiest instrument for the healing of all the world is the union of all its peoples in one universal Cause, one common Faith.[161]

It is not, therefore, in providing support, nor encouragement, nor even example that the work of the Cause chiefly lies. The Bahá'í community will go on contributing in every way possible to efforts toward global unification and social betterment, but such contributions are secondary to its purpose. Its purpose is to assist the people of the world to open their minds and hearts to the one Power that can fulfil their ultimate longing. There are none, except those who have themselves awakened to the Revelation of God, who can bring this help. There are none who can offer credible testimony to a coming world of peace and justice but those who understand, however dimly, the words with which the Voice of God summoned Bahá'u'lláh to arise and undertake His mission:

> Canst thou discover any one but Me, O Pen, in this Day? What hath become of the creation and the manifestations thereof? What of the names and their kingdom? Whither are gone all created things, whether seen or unseen? What of the hidden secrets of the universe and its revelations? Lo, the entire creation hath passed away! Nothing remaineth except My Face, the Ever-Abiding, the Resplendent, the All-Glorious.

> This is the Day whereon naught can be seen except the splendors of the Light that shineth from the face of Thy Lord, the Gracious, the

Most Bountiful. Verily, We have caused every soul to expire by virtue of Our irresistible and all-subduing sovereignty. We have, then, called into being a new creation, as a token of Our grace unto men. I am, verily, the All-Bountiful, the Ancient of Days.[162]

NOTES

1 Shoghi Effendi, *Advent of Divine Justice* (Wilmette: Bahá'í Publishing Trust, 1990), p. 81.

2 Shoghi Effendi, *The Promised Day is Come* (Wilmette: Bahá'í Publishing Trust, 1996), p. 1.

3 Eric Hobsbawm, *Age of Extremes: The Short Twentieth Century, 1914-1991* (London: Abacus, 1995), p. 584.

4 Leopold II, King of the Belgians, operated the colony as a private preserve for some three decades (1877-1908). The atrocities carried out under his misrule aroused international protest, and in 1908 he was compelled to surrender the territory to the administration of the Belgian government.

5 The processes that brought about these changes are reviewed in some detail by A. N. Wilson, et al., *God's Funeral* (London: John Murray, 1999). In 1872, a book published by Winwood Reade under the title *The Martyrdom of Man* (London: Pemberton Publishing, 1968), which became something of a secular "Bible" in the early decades of the twentieth century, expressed the confidence that "finally, men will master the forces of Nature. They will become themselves architects of systems, manufacturers of worlds. Man will then be perfect; he will then be a creator; he will therefore be what the vulgar worship as a god." Cited by Anne Glyn-Jones, *Holding up a Mirror: How Civilizations Decline* (London: Century, 1996), pp. 371-372.

6 *Selections from the Writings of 'Abdu'l-Bahá* (Wilmette: Bahá'í Publishing Trust, 1997), p. 35, (section 15.6).

[7] 'Abdu'l-Bahá, *The Secret of Divine Civilization* (Wilmette: Bahá'í Publishing Trust, 1990), p. 2.

[8] *Makátíb-i-'Abdu'l-Bahá* (Tablets of 'Abdu'l-Bahá), vol. 4 (Tehran: Iran National Publishing Trust, 1965), pp. 132-134, provisional translation.

[9] *ibid.*

[10] *ibid.*

[11] The school was closed in 1934, by order of Reza Shah, because it had observed Bahá'í Holy Days as religious holidays. The closing of all other Bahá'í schools in Iran followed.

[12] See *The Bahá'í World*, vol. XIV (Haifa: Bahá'í World Centre, 1975), pp. 479-481, for history.

[13] Shoghi Effendi, *The World Order of Bahá'u'lláh* (Wilmette: Bahá'í Publishing Trust, 1991), p. 156.

[14] "The outermost circle in this vast system, the visible counterpart of the pivotal position conferred on the Herald of our Faith, is none other than the entire planet. Within the heart of this planet lies the 'Most Holy Land,' acclaimed by 'Abdu'l-Bahá as 'the Nest of the Prophets' and which must be regarded as the center of the world and the Qiblih of the nations. Within this Most Holy Land rises the Mountain of God of immemorial sanctity, the Vineyard of the Lord, the Retreat of Elijah, Whose return the Báb Himself symbolizes. Reposing on the breast of this holy mountain are the extensive properties permanently dedicated to, and constituting the sacred precincts of, the Báb's holy Sepulcher. In the midst of these properties, recognized as the international endowments of the Faith, is situated the most holy court, an enclosure comprising gardens and terraces which at once embellish, and lend a peculiar charm to, these sacred precincts. Embosomed in these lovely and verdant surroundings stands in all its exquisite beauty the mausoleum of the Báb, the shell designed to preserve and adorn the original structure raised by 'Abdu'l-Bahá as the tomb of the Martyr-Herald of our Faith. Within this shell is enshrined that Pearl of Great Price, the holy of holies, those chambers which constitute the tomb itself, and which were constructed by 'Abdu'l-Bahá. Within the heart of this holy of holies is the tabernacle, the vault wherein reposes the most holy casket. Within this vault rests the alabaster sarcophagus in which is deposited that inestimable jewel, the Báb's holy dust." Shoghi Effendi, *Citadel of Faith* (Wilmette: Bahá'í Publishing Trust, 1995), pp. 95-96.

[15] *ibid.*, p. 95.

[16] Shoghi Effendi, *God Passes By* (Wilmette: Bahá'í Publishing Trust, 1995), p. 276.

[17] H. M. Balyuzi, *'Abdu'l-Bahá: The Centre of the Covenant of Bahá'u'lláh*, 2nd ed. (Oxford: George Ronald, 1992), p. 136.

[18] *Selections from the Writings of 'Abdu'l-Bahá, op. cit.*, pp. 254-255, (section 200.3).

[19] Shoghi Effendi, *God Passes By, op. cit.,* p. 258.

[20] *ibid.,* p. 259.

[21] *The Bahá'í Centenary, 1844-1944*, compiled by the National Spiritual Assembly of the Bahá'ís of the United States and Canada (Wilmette: Bahá'í Publishing Committee, 1944), pp. 140-141.

[22] Shoghi Effendi, *God Passes By, op. cit.,* p. 280.

[23] *'Abdu'l-Bahá in London: Addresses and Notes of Conversations* (London: Bahá'í Publishing Trust, 1982), pp. 19-20.

[24] 'Abdu'l-Bahá, *Tablets of the Divine Plan* (Wilmette: Bahá'í Publishing Trust, 1993), p. 94.

[25] Shoghi Effendi, *God Passes By, op. cit.,* pp. 281-282.

[26] 'Abdu'l-Bahá, *The Promulgation of Universal Peace* (Wilmette: Bahá'í Publishing Trust, 1995), p. 121, provisional re-translation.

[27] *Selections From the Writings of 'Abdu'l-Bahá, op. cit.,* p. 106, (section 64.1).

[28] *ibid.,* p. 23, (section 7.2).

[29] 'Abdu'l-Bahá, *The Promulgation of Universal Peace, op. cit.,* pp. 455-456.

[30] Juliet Thompson, *The Diary of Juliet Thompson* (Los Angeles: Kalimát Press, 1983), p. 313.

[31] Shoghi Effendi, *God Passes By, op. cit.,* pp. 244-245.

[32] *Bahá'í World Faith* (Wilmette: Bahá'í Publishing Trust, 1976), p. 429.

[33] *'Abdu'l-Bahá in Canada* (Forest: National Spiritual Assembly of Canada, 1962), p. 51.

[34] 'Abdu'l-Bahá, *Paris Talks*, 12th ed. (London: Bahá'í Publishing Trust, 1995), p. 64.

[35] Eric Hobsbawm, *Age of Extremes: The Short Twentieth Century, 1914-1991, op. cit.,* p. 23.

[36] *Gleanings from the Writings of Bahá'u'lláh* (Wilmette: Bahá'í Publishing Trust, 1983), p. 264, (section CXXV).

[37] Edward R. Kantowicz, *The Rage of Nations* (Cambridge: William B. Eerdmans Publishing Company, 1999), p. 138. Kantowicz adds that the total population loss for Europe was 48 million, including 15 million "swept away" because their run down health made them vulnerable to the post-war influenza epidemic, and because of the reduction caused by the steep drop in the birth rate consequent on these disasters. Hobsbawm estimates that France lost almost twenty percent of its men of military age, Britain lost one quarter of its Oxford and Cambridge graduates who served in the army during the war, while German losses reached 1.8 million or thirteen percent of their military age population. (See Eric Hobsbawm, *Age of Extremes: The Short Twentieth Century, 1914-1991, op. cit.,* p. 26).

[38] President Wilson has been the subject of many biographies over the years since his death. Three relatively recent biographies are Louis Auchincloss, *Woodrow Wilson* (New York: Viking Penguin, 2000); A. Clements Kendrick, *Woodrow Wilson: World Statesman* (Lawrence: University Press of Kansas, 1987); Thomas J. Knock, *To End All Wars: Woodrow Wilson and the Quest for a New World Order* (Oxford: Oxford University Press, 1992).

[39] 'Abdu'l-Bahá, *The Promulgation of Universal Peace, op. cit.*, p. 305.

[40] Shoghi Effendi, *Citadel of Faith, op. cit.*, p. 32.

[41] *ibid.*, pp. 32-33.

[42] As finally adopted, Article X of the Covenant of the League did not require collective military intervention in cases of aggression but merely stated that "…the Council shall advise upon the means by which this obligation shall be fulfilled."

[43] Shoghi Effendi, *The World Order of Bahá'u'lláh, op. cit.*, pp. 29-30.

[44] Shoghi Effendi, *Citadel of Faith, op. cit.*, pp. 28-29.

[45] *ibid.*, p. 7.

[46] *Selections from the Writings of the Báb* (Haifa: Bahá'í World Centre, 1978), p. 56.

[47] Bahá'u'lláh, *The Kitáb-i-Aqdas: The Most Holy Book* (Wilmette: Bahá'í Publishing Trust, 1993), paragraph 88.

[48] *Tablets of Bahá'u'lláh revealed after the Kitáb-i-Aqdas* (Wilmette: Bahá'í Publishing Trust, 1988), p. 13.

[49] The citation made reference to the value of the Master's "advice" to the British military authorities who were attempting to restore civil life following the overthrow of the Turkish regime in the area, adding that "all his influence has been for good". See Moojan Momen, ed., *The Bábí and Bahá'í Religions, 1844-1944: Some Contemporary Western Accounts* (Oxford: George Ronald, 1981), p. 344.

[50] *The Bahá'í World*, vol. XV (Haifa: Bahá'í World Centre, 1976), p. 132.

[51] Horace Holley, *Religion for Mankind* (London: George Ronald, 1956), pp. 243-244.

[52] *Will and Testament of 'Abdu'l-Bahá* (Wilmette: Bahá'í Publishing Trust, 1991), p. 11.

[53] Shoghi Effendi, *God Passes By, op. cit.*, p. 326.

[54] Shoghi Effendi, *Bahá'í Administration* (Wilmette: Bahá'í Publishing Trust, 1998), p. 15.

[55] Rúḥíyyih Rabbání, *The Priceless Pearl* (London: Bahá'í Publishing Trust, 1969), pp. 121, 123.

[56] Shoghi Effendi, *Bahá'í Administration, op. cit.*, pp. 187-188, 194.

[57] In case after case, the open misbehaviour of Shoghi Effendi's brothers, sisters and cousins left him finally with no alternative but to advise the Bahá'í world that these individuals had violated the Covenant.

[58] Shoghi Effendi, *The World Order of Bahá'u'lláh, op. cit.,* p. 36.

[59] *ibid.,* pp. 42-43.

[60] *ibid.,* p. 202.

[61] *ibid.,* pp. 203-204.

[62] Shoghi Effendi, *The World Order of Bahá'u'lláh, op. cit.,* p. 203.

[63] Shoghi Effendi, *The Advent of Divine Justice, op. cit.,* pp. 90, 19, 85.

[64] Nabíl-i-A'ẓam, *The Dawn-Breakers: Nabíl's Narrative of the Early Days of the Bahá'í Revelation* (Wilmette: Bahá'í Publishing Trust, 1999), pp. 92-94.

[65] Shoghi Effendi, *Bahá'í Administration, op. cit.,* p. 52.

[66] *Selections from the Writings of 'Abdu'l-Bahá, op. cit.,* pp. 85-86, (section 38.5).

[67] Shoghi Effendi, *The World Order of Bahá'u'lláh, op. cit.,* p. 4.

[68] *ibid.,* p. 19.

[69] *Gleanings from the Writings of Bahá'u'lláh, op. cit.,* p. 60, (section XXV).

[70] Shoghi Effendi, *The World Order of Bahá'u'lláh, op. cit.,* p. 19.

[71] *ibid.,* p. 144.

[72] Shoghi Effendi, *God Passes By, op. cit.,* p. 26.

[73] *The Bahá'í World,* vol. X (Wilmette: Bahá'í Publishing Committee, 1949), pp. 142-149, provides a detailed survey of the expansion of the Cause up to the conclusion of the first Seven Year Plan.

[74] Shoghi Effendi, *Messages to Canada,* 2nd ed. (Thornhill: Bahá'í Canada Publications, 1999), p. 114.

[75] Shoghi Effendi, *God Passes By, op. cit.,* p. 365.

[76] *Gleanings from the Writings of Bahá'u'lláh, op. cit.,* p. 200, (section XCIX).

[77] Bahá'u'lláh, *The Kitáb-i-Íqán* (Wilmette: Bahá'í Publishing Trust, 1983), p. 31.

[78] "In Europe at the start of the twentieth century, most people accepted the authority of morality…. [Then] reflective Europeans were also able to believe in moral progress, and to see human viciousness and barbarism as in retreat. At the end of the century, it is hard to be confident either about the moral law or about moral progress": Jonathon Glover, *Humanity: A Moral History of the Twentieth Century* (London: Jonathan Cape, 1999), p. 1. Glover's study concentrates particularly on the rise and influence of twentieth century ideologies.

[79] Shoghi Effendi, *The Promised Day is Come, op. cit.,* pp. 185-186.

[80] *ibid.*

[81] *Gleanings from the Writings of Bahá'u'lláh, op. cit.,* pp. 65-66, (section XXVII).

[82] *ibid.,* pp. 41-42, (section XVII).

[83] *Women: Extracts from the Writings of Bahá'u'lláh, 'Abdu'l-Bahá, Shoghi Effendi and the Universal House of Justice,* compiled by the Research Department of the Universal House of Justice (Thornhill: Bahá'í Canada Publications, 1986), p. 50.

[84] Shoghi Effendi, *Messages to America* (Wilmette: Bahá'í Publishing Committee, 1947), p. 28.

[85] *ibid.,* pp. 9, 10, 14, 22.

[86] *ibid.,* p. 28.

[87] Rúḥíyyih Rabbání, *The Priceless Pearl, op. cit.,* p. 382.

[88] Shoghi Effendi, *Messages to America, op. cit.,* p. 53.

[89] Shoghi Effendi, *The World Order of Bahá'u'lláh, op. cit.,* p. 46.

[90] *'Abdu'l-Bahá in Canada, op. cit.,* p. 51.

[91] 'Abdu'l-Bahá, *The Promulgation of Universal Peace, op. cit.,* p. 377.

[92] 'Abdu'l-Bahá, *Foundations of World Unity* (Wilmette: Bahá'í Publishing Trust, 1979), p. 21.

[93] Lester Bowles Pearson (1897-1972) was awarded the 1957 Nobel prize for peace for his formulation of international policy in the period after World War II, particularly for his plan that led to the establishment of the first United Nations' emergency force in the Suez Canal in 1956, a response to the crisis created by the invasion of Egypt by British and French military forces, acting in agreement with those of Israel, following the seizure of the Suez Canal by Egypt. The first formal vote of international sanctions against aggression, taken in 1936 by the League of Nations, when Fascist Italy invaded Ethiopia, was hailed by Shoghi Effendi as: "an event without parallel in human history". (See Shoghi Effendi, *The World Order of Bahá'u'lláh, op. cit.,* p. 191.)

[94] The three United Nations' Secretaries-General mentioned were, in chronological order, Javier Pérez de Cuellar (1982-1991), Peru; Boutros Boutros-Ghali (1992-96), Egypt; Kofi Annan, (1997-present), Ghana.

[95] Anne Frank (1929-1945) – Jewish youth, victim of Nazi genocide, captured in her family's hiding place in the Netherlands in August 1944 and sent to the concentration camp at Belsen, where she died a year later. Her diary was published in 1952 under the title *The Diary of a Young Girl* and subsequently dramatized on the stage and in film. Martin Luther King Jr. (1929-1968) – American clergyman and Nobel laureate, one of the principal leaders of the American civil rights movement, who was assassinated on 4 April 1968 in Memphis, Tennessee. He is commemorated in the United States in a national holiday on the third Monday of January. Paulo Freire (1921-1997) – innovative Brazilian educator, whose pioneer work in adult education won him international fame, but led to two periods of imprisonment in his own country. Kiri Te Kanawa (1944-) – Born in New Zealand of Maori ancestry, and today one of the world's leading operatic *divas.* Awarded the Order of Dame

Commander of the British Empire by H. M. Queen Elizabeth II, 1982. Gabriel García Marques (1928-) – Colombian writer and novelist, winner of the Nobel prize for literature in 1982, who was compelled to spend the 1960s and 1970s in voluntary exile in Mexico and Spain to escape persecution in his native land. Ravi Shankar (1920-) – Indian composer and sitarist, whose impressive talents and tours of Europe and North America contributed to the awakening of interest in Indian music throughout the West. Andrei Dmitriyevich Sakharov (1921-1989) – Russian nuclear physicist, who abandoned scientific research to become the leading spokesman for civil liberties in the Soviet Union, for which he was awarded the 1975 Nobel Peace Prize, while suffering internal exile in his own land. "Mother Teresa" (Agnes Gonxha Borjaxhiu, 1910-1997) – Albanian born Roman Catholic nun, founder of the Missionaries of Charity, whose self-sacrificing work on behalf of the poor, the homeless and the dying in Calcutta won her the Nobel Peace Prize in 1979. Zhang Yimou (1951-) – A leading director among China's "Fifth Generation" film makers and winner of many professional awards for his sensitive and visually stunning work.

[96] The three new National Spiritual Assemblies were Canada, which established a National Assembly separate from that of the United States in 1948, and the Regional Assemblies of Central America and the Antilles (1951) and South America (1951).

[97] Shoghi Effendi, *Messages to the Bahá'í World, 1950-1957* (Wilmette: Bahá'í Publishing Trust, 1995), p. 41.

[98] *ibid.*, pp. 38-39.

[99] *Will and Testament of 'Abdu'l-Bahá, op. cit.,* p. 13.

[100] Under the leadership of two of 'Abdu'l-Bahá's half brothers, Muḥammad 'Alí and Badí'u'lláh, together with a cousin, Majdi'd-Dín, the group of Covenant-breakers who had long occupied the Mansion at Bahjí after the death of Bahá'u'lláh carried on an unremitting campaign of attacks and machinations against both the Master and the Guardian. Under the British Mandate, they had been forced to evacuate the Mansion because of the neglect into which they had allowed it to fall, thus permitting the Guardian to restore the building and establish its status in the eyes of the civil authorities as a Holy Place. Subsequently, Shoghi Effendi secured from the newly established Israeli government recognition that the entire property had this privileged character, and an official order was issued, requiring the remaining Covenant-breakers to evacuate the unsightly building that they still occupied next to the Mansion. When their appeal to the Supreme Court against this judgement failed, the eviction order was executed, the building demolished at the Guardian's instructions, and the last obstacle to the beautification of the property was successfully overcome.

[101] *Tablets of Bahá'u'lláh revealed after the Kitáb-i-Aqdas, op. cit.,* p. 68.

[102] *Will and Testament of 'Abdu'l-Bahá, op. cit.,* pp. 19-20.

103 A full account of the role played by the Hands of the Cause during these critical years is provided by Amatu'l-Bahá Rúḥíyyih Khánum, *Ministry of the Custodians* (Haifa: Bahá'í World Centre, 1997).

104 Shoghi Effendi, *The World Order of Bahá'u'lláh, op. cit.,* p. 148.

105 *Will and Testament of 'Abdu'l-Bahá, op. cit.,* p. 20.

106 Universal House of Justice, *Messages from the Universal House of Justice, 1963-1986: The Third Epoch of the Formative Age* (Wilmette: Bahá'í Publishing Trust, 1996), p. 14.

107 The subject is discussed in a number of places throughout *The Priceless Pearl, op. cit.* See particularly pages 79, 85, 90, 128 and 159.

108 *Tablets of Bahá'u'lláh revealed after the Kitáb-i-Aqdas, op. cit.,* p. 69.

109 'Abdu'l-Bahá, *The Secret of Divine Civilization, op. cit.,* pp. 96-97.

110 J. E. Esslemont, *Bahá'u'lláh and the New Era: An Introduction to the Bahá'í Faith,* 5th rev. ed. (Wilmette: Bahá'í Publishing Trust, 1998), p. 250.

111 *Will and Testament of 'Abdu'l-Bahá, op. cit.,* p. 11.

112 Shoghi Effendi, *The World Order of Bahá'u'lláh, op. cit.,* p. 8.

113 Bahá'u'lláh, *The Kitáb-i-Aqdas, op. cit.,* paragraph 83.

114 Bahá'u'lláh, *Epistle to the Son of the Wolf* (Wilmette: Bahá'í Publishing Trust, 1988), p. 14.

115 Shoghi Effendi, *The World Order of Bahá'u'lláh, op. cit.,* pp. 43, 195.

116 *ibid.,* p. 24.

117 *Tablets of Bahá'u'lláh revealed after the Kitáb-i-Aqdas, op. cit.,* pp. 66-67.

118 Shoghi Effendi, *The Advent of Divine Justice, op. cit.,* p. 27.

119 *The Establishment of the Universal House of Justice,* compiled by the Research Department of the Universal House of Justice (Oakham: Bahá'í Publishing Trust, 1984), p. 17.

120 Universal House of Justice, *Messages from the Universal House of Justice, 1963-1986: The Third Epoch of the Formative Age, op. cit.,* p. 52.

121 *ibid,* p. 104.

122 *Bahá'í News,* no. 73, May 1933 (Wilmette: National Spiritual Assembly of the Bahá'ís of the United States), p. 7.

123 The Institute was created by the Universal House of Justice in 1998 as an agency of the Bahá'í International Community, reporting to the House of Justice through the Office of Public Information. Its mandate describes it as an agency "dedicated to researching both the spiritual and material underpinnings of human knowledge and the processes of social advancement."

[124] The Centre's purpose is described as undertaking "research in a systematic manner on the Bahá'í Faith, including its religious culture, humanitarian spirit and religious ethics."

[125] Cited in *Star of the West,* vol. 13, no. 7 (October 1922), pp. 184-186.

[126] 'Abdu'l-Bahá, *Tablets of the Divine Plan, op. cit.,* p. 54.

[127] Beginning in approximately 1904, a learned Iranian believer known as Ṣadru'ṣ-Ṣudúr established the first teacher-training class for Bahá'í youth in Tehran with 'Abdu'l-Bahá's encouragement. The classes met daily, and the graduates, who had been trained in the beliefs of other religions as well as various aspects of the Bahá'í Faith, contributed greatly to the expansion and consolidation of the Cause in their native land.

[128] The model in question is the "Ruhi Institute", whose materials and methods have been adopted by many Bahá'í communities throughout the world. Its guiding philosophy is an integration of service activities with focused study of the Bahá'í Writings themselves. Organized as a series of levels of study, which form a central "trunk" of basic understanding of the spiritual essentials taught by Bahá'u'lláh, the system allows for the almost infinite development by various user communities of branching subsets that serve particular needs.

[129] Shoghi Effendi, *God Passes By, op. cit.,* p. xiii.

[130] 'Abdu'l-Bahá, *The Promulgation of Universal Peace, op. cit.,* pp. 43-44.

[131] Moojan Momen, *The Babí and Bahá'í Religions, 1844-1944: Some Contemporary Western Accounts, op. cit.,* pp. 186-187.

[132] *The Bahá'í World,* vol. XV, *op. cit.,* pp. 29, 36.

[133] *The Bahá'í World,* vol. IV (New York City: Bahá'í Publishing Committee, 1933), pp. 257-261. Provides a short history of the bureau's founding and operations.

[134] *The Bahá'í World,* vol. III (New York City: Bahá'í Publishing Committee, 1930), pp. 198-206. Contains the text of a formal Petition to the Permanent Mandates Commission of the League from the Bahá'ís of Iraq, that summarizes the history of the case.

[135] Shoghi Effendi, *God Passes By, op. cit.,* p. 360.

[136] The full text of the Declaration may be found in *World Order Magazine,* April 1947, vol. XIII, No. 1.

[137] *The Bahá'í Question, Iran's Secret Blueprint for the Destruction of a Religious Community, An Examination of the Persecution of the Bahá'ís of Iran* (New York: Bahá'í International Community, 1999), prepared by the Bahá'í International Community United Nations' Office for distribution to members of the United Nations Human Rights Commission.

[138] Excerpt from an address by Edward Granville Browne, published in *Religious Systems of the World: A Contribution to the Study of Comparative Religion,* 3rd ed. (New York: Macmillan, 1892), pp. 352-353.

[139] During the nine years of its existence, the office was responsible for settling an estimated 10,000 Iranian Bahá'í refugees in twenty-seven countries.

[140] To date, ninety-nine National Spiritual Assemblies have received intensive training in the programme.

[141] The Beijing Conference on Women would have permitted fifty out of the two thousand non-governmental organizations involved to present their statements orally. Because the Bahá'í International Community had received this privilege at previous conferences, most notably that in Rio de Janeiro on the environment and that in Copenhagen on social and economic development, the Community's representatives yielded the slot that had been accorded them, in favour of the Moscow Centre for Gender Studies.

[142] A full account, including the text of the decision of the German Federal Constitutional Court, can be found in *The Bahá'í World*, vol. XX (Haifa: Bahá'í World Centre, 1998), pp. 571-606.

[143] *Sessão Solene da Câmara Federal*, Brasília, 28 de Maio, 1992, (reprinted, with English translation by the National Spiritual Assembly of the Bahá'ís of Brazil, 1992).

[144] *Selections from the Writings of 'Abdu'l-Bahá, op. cit.*, pp. 34-36, (section 15).

[145] United Nations General Assembly, *Fifty-Fourth Session, Agenda Item 49 (b) United Nations Reform Measures and Proposals: the Millennium Assembly of the United Nations*, 8 August 2000, (Document no. A/54/959), p. 2.

[146] See *Commitment to Global Peace*, declaration of the Millennium World Peace Summit of Religious and Spiritual Leaders, presented to UN Secretary-General Kofi Annan on 29 August 2000 during a summit session at the UN General Assembly.

[147] United Nations General Assembly, *Fifty-Fourth Session, Agenda Item 61 (b) The Millennium Assembly of the United Nations*, 8 September 2000, (Document no. A/55/L.2), section 32.

[148] The respective purposes of the three Millennium gatherings, as well as the involvement of the Bahá'í community in these meetings, were summarized in a letter from the Universal House of Justice to all National Spiritual Assemblies dated 24 September 2000.

[149] Shoghi Effendi, *The World Order of Bahá'u'lláh, op. cit.*, p. 42.

[150] *Gleanings from the Writings of Bahá'u'lláh, op. cit.*, p. 297, (section CXXXVI).

[151] Bahá'u'lláh, *The Kitáb-i-Íqán, op. cit.*, p. 34.

[152] Bahá'u'lláh, *Prayers and Meditations* (Wilmette: Bahá'í Publishing Trust, 1998), p. 295, (section CLXXVIII).

[153] Shoghi Effendi, *The World Order of Bahá'u'lláh, op. cit.*, p. 193.

[154] *ibid.*, p. 196.

[155] Bahá'u'lláh, *The Kitáb-i-Aqdas, op. cit.,* paragraph 186.

[156] *ibid.,* paragraph 54.

[157] Shoghi Effendi, *Messages to the Bahá'í World, 1950-1957, op. cit.,* p. 74.

[158] Isaiah 2.2 Authorized (King James) Version.

[159] Shoghi Effendi, *The Advent of Divine Justice, op. cit.,* pp. 82-83.

[160] *Selections from the Writings of 'Abdu'l-Bahá, op. cit.,* p. 317, (section 227.22).

[161] *The Proclamation of Bahá'u'lláh* (Haifa: Bahá'í World Centre, 1967), p. 67.

[162] *Gleanings from the Writings of Bahá'u'lláh, op. cit.,* pp. 29-30, (section XIV).

INDEX

social and economic development, 103, 105

social progress, 8

Some Answered Questions, 66

Soviet Union, 61–62, 88, 89

S.S. Himalaya, 29

Stalin, Josef, 62

Stannard, Jean, 115

steadfastness, 18

study circles, 110

Sudan, National Spiritual Assembly of, 57

Suez Canal, 152n. 93

Sun Yat-sen, 44

Sydney (Australia), House of Worship in, 79

T

Tablet of Carmel, 36, 141–42

Tablets of the Divine Plan

  'Abdu'l-Bahá and, 36

  youth and, 109

  See also Divine Plan

Ṭáhirih, 100

Tanumafili, His Highness Malietoa II, of Samoa, 99

Tarbíyat school, 11, 148n. 11

teaching, 99–100, 110

Tehran, Spiritual Assembly of, 56

Te Kanawa, Kiri, 74, 152–53n. 95

tempest of change, 2

Temple Emanu-El, 22

Temple Unity Board, 57

Ten Year Crusade (Spiritual Crusade, 1953–1963), 77–79, 97, 139

Teresa, Mother, 74, 153n. 95

Thailand, 124

theory of relativity, 5

"Third World," 88

Thompson, Juliet, 26, 66

Three Year Plan (1993–1996), 98

training institutes, 110, 155n. 128

True, Corinne, 66

Turkestan, House of Worship in 'Ishqábád, 13, 23, 56

Twelve Month Plan (2000–2001), 98

twentieth century, 52

twentieth century *(continued)*

  as century of light, 8–9, 22, 127

  transformation of society in, 1, 137–38

U

Uganda

  Bahá'í community of, 106

  House of Worship in Kampala, 77, 79

  teaching in, 100

United Nations, 91

  "A Bahá'í Declaration on Human Obligations and Rights" and, 116

  Bahá'í International Community and, 116, 122–24, 129–30

  Children's Fund (UNICEF), 116–17

  Commission on Human Rights, 73

  Conference of Non-Governmental Organizations, 123

  conferences of, 123–24

  Economic and Social Council (ECOSOC), 116

  Environmental Programme (UNEP), 116

  establishment of, 71–72

  Executive Committee of Non-Governmental Organizations, 123

  High Commission for Refugees, 120

  Human Development Report (1999), 134

  Human Rights Commission, 119, 121

  human rights system of, 121–22

  millennium events of, 129–31, 132, 134

  "Palestine Committee," 115–16

  Secretary-Generals of, 74, 152n. 94

  Third Committee of General Assembly, 119

  Universal Declaration of Human Rights, 119, 121

United States

  'Abdu'l-Bahá in, 20–21, 22–23, 71–72

  community, destiny of, 34, 67

  League of Nations and, 35

  National Spiritual Assembly of, 57

  teachers in, 100

  See also individual names of cities in.